#7

cp

H2

D1295710

MEMORIES
OF
ARLINGTON, VERMONT

Memories
of
Arlington, Vermont

by DOROTHY CANFIELD FISHER

DUELL, SLOAN AND PEARCE

New York

First Edition

Acknowledgment is made to Harcourt, Brace and
Company, Inc., for "The Washed Window" from
A Harvest of Stories, copyright, 1955, by Dorothy
Canfield Fisher. Twenty sections of this book were
first published as *Memories of My Home Town,*
privately printed in 1955 for the Arlington Historical
Society. Two sections, "The Washed Window" and
"The Soldier's Return," have appeared in *American
Heritage.*

Library of Congress Catalog Card No. 57-11058

MANUFACTURED IN THE UNITED STATES OF AMERICA

VAN REES PRESS • NEW YORK

TO

The People of Arlington,
of the Past,
of the Present, and of the Future

The Purpose
of This Series

Some of the memories set down in this volume have been for nearly two centuries living in human minds, invisible to any reading eye. Some of them date from only last year. To us Arlington people they seem like old familiar friends, summoned up from the past, near or long ago, in well-remembered voices.

It was a surprise to us—we almost fancifully feel it must have surprised these local memories—when, a year ago, some of them were printed in a little book as part of the effort of our local Historical Society to preserve a reasonable amount, not only of the facts of our communal past, but of its human color, too. And we were as much startled as pleased when all copies of the small volume were sold before we could draw our comfortably slow, rural breath. Walter Hard, our book-selling cousin and neighbor in near-by Manchester, made a phrase about it, remarking that that Arlington book "became a collector's item before it was off the printing press."

Time went on. The horizon lifted above the mountain walls which enclose our Arlington. We began to feel that not only people at the other end of our valley are our neighbors. All Americans are. In this huge Union of diverse States, aren't we all moving out from under our old regional horizons to the lofty, spacious, total arch of a national sky?

Not just politically. That was done in the late eighteenth century in Philadelphia, by our Founding Fathers. Humanly. We have always known that we are one huge nation. Now, more and more, we are learning to feel it.

In our times, nobody needs to be reminded that we draw from such a federation as that of our United States of America, incalculable material benefits. I don't suppose there is one American living who thinks it might have been better for our nation to be made up of independent States, each one on its own, walled in by frontier barriers as in Europe.

The political, economic and industrial advantages of national unity, so visible to us, so taken for granted, are enormous. But from the human point of view, there are disadvantages. In the nature of things, a federation must be bigger than any of its member units. In the United States of America, the federation of all our combined States is so big, so various, and so incredibly diversified that it is hard for people in any one region fully to realize that people in a distant corner of the Federation are really *neighbors,* in the richly flesh-and-blood meaning of the word, just like the families who live next door, or on the same block. The catch is that you know your geographical neighbors in shared daily life, as you do not at all know your voting comrades in the political organization of a federation.

Well, if we are all to be fully fellow-countrymen, we'd better set about knowing each other more humanly. The purpose of this series of home-town memories is a move in this direction. Each one of the books in this series has as its intention—to give the reader some informal glimpses of the homely human life of a region not his own.

DOROTHY CANFIELD FISHER

Arlington, Vermont
Spring, 1957

Contents

LATER NINETEENTH CENTURY AND
TWENTIETH CENTURY

MEMORIES
OF
ARLINGTON, VERMONT

A Look Around
Our Mountain Town

In Arlington, as in most small, old, close-knit communities, everyday chat between neighbors is not limited to the present. The past is a part of today. Especially if a piece of the past is, as old stories often are, an explanatory footnote from 1810, or 1799, or 1862, or 1955, to gossip of the day marked on your calendar as now.

These stories are so familiar to us who cite them that often we need to use only a single phrase, as, "Who's sick?" or, "Where's my hat?" or, "Can't leave my horses." They are like the "story of the grouse in the gun room" in *She Stoops to Conquer,* that is, to us they are not in the least dependent on being new. Modern, invented tales or anecdotes for television or vaudeville cannot be told twice in talk, because many of them have no value beyond the unexpectedness of the crack at the end. We treasure our remembered people and doings after repeated hearings because they are comments on human life, drawn from somebody's first-hand experience in living. For us they do not get forlornly cracked and shabby with much handling, but are rather like a well-kept, much-used old pine table or maple desk, come down from our community's past, with a gleam—"patina" is the stylish name given to this quality—which only age and constant, purposeful use can produce.

At first we had thought that these memories from the life of our plain old home town should be kept, like our plain old pine tables, right where they have always been. It had seemed to us that an incommunicable part of their flavor comes from the fact that they have a geographical tie to this particular valley where they happened. And yet, we do notice that our ancient pine tables and chairs are often valued and cherished by people not geographically connected with them. Perhaps these homely anecdotes, these blades of grass plucked from the thousands growing in our mountain meadow, may also be valued by others. Maybe that meadow is not just ours, but yours, too.

But before you begin to look at one blade of grass after another (not too many at one time, I hope), you ought to have a look around the meadow.

If you stepped off the bus which goes through Arlington from Albany to Montreal, what would you see? You'd see a long valley between two ranges of green mountains. Colorado and Wyoming people laugh at our calling them "mountains," for they are seldom more than 3,000 feet high. They seem high to us because the valley is rather narrow, and the mountains on each side make us lift our eyes to see the sun rising behind their rim on the eastern side, or setting behind the range on the western side. But I remember a distant cousin of the Canfields, who had always lived in Nebraska, came here one summer to visit the Vermont old folks—just to see what kind of a place her grandfather and grandmother had come from. We were astonished by her exclaiming as she looked around, "I don't see how you breathe here—the mountains are so close and shut off so much of the sky, I feel when I glance up quickly from sewing or reading as though they were going to fall on me."

To think that our mild Green Mountains with their suave flowing lines could make anybody think them imprisoning! Of course what that exclamation of people who come in from prairie land does for us, is to make us imagine much more vividly than any book description the wide, level spaciousness of the prairie country, with the whole bowl of the sky visible. It has helped us to lift our eyes beyond the Vermont borders, and to realize visually that we are Americans, as well as Vermonters. Perhaps this glimpse into our green valley may help a Nebraska cousin to lift her eyes from the prairies and realize that Vermont is hers, also.

When you look at the outside of a landscape new to you, you see it as the picture-postcard photographer sees it—just the surface. What I'm trying to do in these preliminary words is to give you some idea of what that surface has meant to the people who have lived on it. The surface has changed greatly from time to time. The people, and their way of taking life, have not changed much.

Here's an example. Our mountains are now covered with trees up to the very top. But they were not always so. Arlington was settled by people from western Connecticut in the middle of the eighteenth century, 1764 to be exact. At that time no ordinary person in the British colonies had so much as heard of the rich prairie lands to the west. They came mostly from the British Islands where cultivatable land had been the foundation of society because you could grow food on it. Our ancestors, the New England younger generation who first came into this valley, were like all other eighteenth-century British colonists—they considered the first duty of all new settlers in any country to "create" as much open land as possible by cutting down the trees. With energy they felled the trees as far as possible up the steep slopes of the mountains. Where in the 1760's pine and hemlocks and oak and maples had stood, our forefathers, very well satisfied with themselves, saw, in the early nineteenth century, sloping meadows and pastures and the occasional more or less flat places, well plowed, harrowed, cultivated, growing food—and wide-open to erosion.

About that time, say, from 1810 on, the news began to get around that 'way out West, in the far part of York State, there were broad flat acres of rich farm-land open to settling. Then began the movement away from Vermont towards the newly opened regions—western New York at first, then the fabulously rich soil of the middle states, and then on to beautiful, fertile Iowa. Like most other Vermont towns, Arlington was never emptied and abandoned. The number of people living here was always about the same. But it no longer grew in population. The first really static and stable element appeared in our communal life, which in its economic ways has transformed itself in the course of almost every generation.

By the early 1850's, the railroad was running. The shining steel tracks ran along the bottom of our valley like so many magnets, drawing down to them the people who had been living contentedly far up on the mountain shelves. With those steel tracks began the modern way of producing manufactured goods. And of transporting them to larger markets.

The beehive hum of spinning wheels was replaced by factory whistles. The early team of sixteen sweating, panting horses, tugging their hearts out to pull over muddy roads the cruelly heavy loads of marble from the small quarries around Arlington down to the Hudson River at Troy and Albany, vanished, even as my great-grandmother wrung her hands to see the suffering of the horses. The shrieking railroad, its whistle re-echoing from the mountains, carried on one freight car as much as many of the big horse-drawn wagons.

For a while the felling of trees went on even more rapidly than ever, because it was now possible to ship them out by railway to parts of the Federation which didn't have, like Vermont, more trees than they knew what to do with. Except in the steepest slopes, the mountains in Vermont were becoming denuded. As early as in the 1820's, Vermonters began to cry calamity, as human beings are apt to do, over a great change of which they could see only one corner. There was a lamentation over cutting down for lumber the big sugar-maple trees when they could make maple syrup, so useful, so much a part of the business of our State. There was also a wail over the abandoning of small communities, up on mountain shelves, or on the flat cols which connect one mountain with another. It is always a shock to older people to see the homes of their youth forsaken and desolate. Their younger generation had moved down into the valley, nearer the railroads, where there was much more paid employment available.

The old people looked back with homesickness to the past, which to old people is always so much happier than the present. For them the past was the almost medieval way of self-sufficient life up there on the higher slopes and levels. How happy we were when we lived up there, the old people were saying. Their young folks were meanwhile reveling in valley life—for by this time the beaver swamps had been drained and roads ran everywhere in the valley. Neighbors were near, the doctor was available for the sick, there was paid work in factories, mail coming in every day (almost!), schools near enough so that every child could attend without too much effort, and modern luxuries like kitchen stoves where you could stand up comfortably to cook, replacing the old yawning fireplaces where you stooped and squatted to turn the pancakes.

Arlington rearranged itself around the railroad and the factories like crystals forming in their orderly way, orderly and ever repeating, in a glass full of salt-saturated water. Transportation of all kinds of goods disappeared from the roads, and so did the great herds of cattle which, at certain seasons, had crowded the muddy or dusty roads leading towards Boston or Albany and the Hudson. How well I remember those huge traveling herds on their way to market, which blocked the roads at certain times of the year, and made a delicious excitement for children. Now the valley roads between the towns were almost empty except for occasional farmers jogging into town to get the mail, to trade eggs for exotic products like tobacco.

Once again a stable, to-the-eye unchanging way of life settled down over the valley. Young folks grumbled "nothing ever changes here." With peaceful contentment elderly people began to make the same comment. The comings and goings of trains to and from our railway station felt as set as the hours when the sun rose and sank. Arlington set its clocks by the whistle of the morning train "down"—that is, south to York State and the Hudson—or "up"—that is, towards Canada and Montreal. The pattern seemed fixed. The surface looked absolutely stable—our villages with their churches, their well-kept homes and lawns, their old burying grounds —you'd think what many people used to say then as they do now, "Does anything ever change here?" If you could see a speeded-up history of this stable Vermont mountain town you would see a whirl of change sweeping each human generation to new positions in the valley, in the mountains, in life, in occupation.

Motor cars shook up the kaleidoscope once more. A new pattern began to form out of the same old pieces—young folks, old folks, children, babies. That's the stable element of our life, we now see, not the surface but the people who live here, people working for their livings. There were fewer daily trains; and then, to our consternation, no passenger trains at all. But by that time the horseless buggies had stopped seeming funny. They were no longer carrying erratically and uncertainly a few eccentrics here and there, for fun. An ever-thickening line of business-like automobiles filled the old highways, and carried people and then goods more swiftly and more directly than ever before to their destinations. Big trucks appeared, manufacturing changed, manufactured products were carried away in trucks, grain was brought in from the West where it was produced more cheaply than was possible in the small stone-walled fields of Vermont, farming changed, older people were dismayed—all over again—at the exodus of the young people. Still, Arlington had just about as many inhabitants as ever.

Drop the eyes of your imagination from this whirl of change, this ever-repeated adjustment to modern life as it rushes forward. What do you see here now? You see a settlement which has in it almost precisely the same number of people that it had in the last half of the eighteenth century when all this began. There are now a little less than fifteen hundred inhabitants here in Arlington, and that's just what there was when the first census was taken in the eighteenth century. There have been constant shifts in the location of homes and in the work done—but these shifts have taken about one generation each to happen.

We think it meaningful that many of our institutions have not vanished or changed like the material framework of life, that the quality of daily life here has, we think, improved. In 1806, a hundred and fifty years ago, there was a public library here much valued by the people. There were perhaps a hundred and fifty books in it. We have a public library now, a successor of that, which has grown to five thousand volumes.

From the earliest eighteenth-century days, every Arlington child has had some form of education. There was practically no illiteracy then, and there is practically none now. But the education which our children are receiving is much better.

When I say that the population is just about the same, I don't mean that the people here are the lineal descendants, without exception, of the same people who were here in 1790. Our town records have been kept systematically and legibly. Through them, backing up our communal memory, we can see pretty well what has been happening to the people of our town. As to racial origin, I mean. To begin with, 100 per cent of Arlington people were old English-speaking stock. You can tell that from their names—Hall, Washburn, Lathrop, Freeman, Pettibone, Barnes, Oatman, Fuller and so forth. Many of those names no longer appear in Arlington except on old tombstones. But some of them still do, borne by rosy, bouncing, quick-witted girls and boys racing in and out of the big, consolidated modern school which has taken the place of all those many scattered one-room district schools.

Some years ago, we were having a celebration at our high school, in honor of some mural paintings of early days here which were to be unveiled. The committee in charge of planning the program suggested uncertainly, "Perhaps we could find enough children in the school here who are descendants of the first settlers of 1764, to act as symbols and stand up on the platform and draw the curtains aside." Nobody knew whether there still were any school children who were descendants of the original settlers. There turned out to be more than we could find room for on the platform.

After having been a Vermont settlement, Arlington has become an American town. After having been of 100 per cent English-speaking origin, by 1850, 88 per cent of the people here were of that stock. By 1850, the railroad had been built, men fresh from Ireland helped build it, and with their families had settled along its line. Their children were growing up as Arlington young folks. By 1888, 73 per cent of the people here were of old English stock. By 1950, 56 per cent of them were of old English stock; 13 per cent were Irish; 17 per cent had come in from north Europe—Finns (such fine citizens we have had from Finland), Swedes, Danes and so forth; 6 per cent were French from French Canada; 6 per cent were new from Scotland; 2 per cent were Italian. And—take it from me—all of them are Arlington folks. The older generation has been terrified by each change as it happened. They were tragically sure that our town would be transformed into something different. But each new generation found it no more and no less than just Arlington. By the latest census Arlington has—well, I forget whether four, or six, or fifteen more or fewer people than it had at the time of the American Revolution. That is, it has stability. But an American kind of stability, made up not of stagnation and immobility, but of constant rediscovery of stable elements in a shifting community life—churches, books, education, civic responsibility, shared good times, neighborly feeling, a solidarity which makes everybody feel safe.

Not having changed the number of its inhabitants, Arlington is still small enough so that nearly everybody knows everybody else, at least by sight, and feels him as a human, not merely a political and economic member of the community. We know we are acquainted not only with the people who live here now, but with those who have lived here long ago, because of just such memories as are set down in this collection.

I'll give an example. On the exact location of one of the garages on our Main Street, a blacksmith shop used to stand. I remember it very well. Like most blacksmith shops, it was a place of gathering for all kinds of people, some who came to have their horses shod, or a pair of andirons repaired, some who had just come to sit around and talk. A little Morgan horse had been given to me by a great-uncle, so I often had a reason for going there. The blacksmith was a massive, muscular man, one of the Conroys. Irish you see. His parents had been born in Ireland. In those days, blacksmithing was a skilled occupation. No town could keep house without a good one. The grandfather of Senator Taft was a blacksmith "just over the mountain" from us here. He was also the President of the Trustees of the Townshend Seminary there.

Our Dennis Conroy, the blacksmith, was not only admired as a skilled worker in iron (one of the oldest skills known to humanity) but highly esteemed as a substantial member of society. For many years he was a member of the local board of school directors. All the skills which were practiced in that shop were familiar, seventy years ago—how to weight a horse's shoes on the outer edge so the horse wouldn't cut the ankle on the opposite foot at any gait, how to cure saddle sores, how to use a martingale for a young horse to keep him from rearing, and of course how to keep a horse clean—all those skills are now as completely outdated as the use of the spinning wheel. So of course the blacksmith shop is gone. If we could see the passing generations of our town in that shortened perspective of the speeded-up picture of the moving picture, we would see the blacksmith shop, once filled with useful activity, whirled up by the tornado of change like a spark from a bonfire, and vanishing forever. And so, sadly, our oldest generation are apt to see it for they are saddened by change as if it were death.

But it isn't. Old Dennis Conroy had a son. He had none of his father's manual skill with shaping iron. He knew no more about shoeing a horse than you do. But he had other skills, suitable for the time he was born into. When he grew up to earn his living, he ran a garage, repaired automobiles and sold them. He was as useful to Arlington as ever his father had been.

That son had a son and he has no mechanical aptitudes. Here is his story as far as it has gone, for he's still a young man with two young children. Earning every cent of his expenses except what he got free from Arlington's good-quality primary and high school and later from the G.I. Bill of Rights, he went through Antioch College, got an M.A. from the University of Chicago later, went to Washington (against everybody's advice) to try to find some work with the State Department, because he had become much interested in international affairs. He is now in Ethiopia doing important and responsible work in the Point Four Program. But there are still plenty of garages on our Main Street, where automobiles are repaired and sold. The work of the men who run these garages is valued and respected as much as the blacksmith's ever was, and for the same reason, because it is essentially useful, and their owners and managers are respected for the same reason, because they are good citizens.

Since Arlington is full as it always has been of human beings, every house on every street has been the background for some kind of human story, a success story, a failure story. But you will not find here one of the traditional success stories common in American lore—the boy who started life as a bootblack, and grew up to be a great financier. As far as I can find out, no financier so much as slept overnight in our town, and there never has been a bootblack in Arlington. Everybody here during two hundred years (almost) has blackened his own shoes.

There are, in that passing look into three generations of the Conroy family, no sociological words or abstract conceptions. But I think it tells you something about the kind of town Arlington is, something you would not know if you walked up and down our village street while the tank of your car was taking in gasoline from a local filling station. You'd probably say—most passers-by do, "What fine old elms along this street! And look, white marble slabs for sidewalks!" Sometimes we think we should put up a neat little notice, "We use marble for our sidewalks because, when they were made early in the 1800's, no such thing as concrete existed, and local quarries made marble the cheapest stone we could use." But perhaps sociologically and historically considered, the really interesting thing about our sidewalks is that a poor mountain town where everybody scrabbled hard and steadily for his living voted sidewalks for itself at Town Meeting early in the 1800's. And here they still are.

I suppose I ought to tell you in this report something about the way we are governed. Like all other Vermont towns, Arlington is—always has been—governed not by representatives, but directly, by its citizens. Every voter in town—that now means all women, too—assembles on Town Meeting Day, to talk over and argue about what must be done to get our community through the year which faces us. We ourselves decide, by our votes, the amount of taxes we will pay during the next year. Enough money must be raised to keep up the roads, provide for the schools, take care of those among the poor and sick and old who haven't money to take care of themselves, keep the bridges sound for these heavy new trucks which now keep thundering through town, take action about such a new catastrophe as gypsy moths in our trees—in short, meet the familiar, ever-recurrent, very diverse problems of a community. Not to speak of the new ones which occasionally burst explosively in our midst.

At Town Meeting, every voter is expected to speak up if he has something he wants his fellow-citizens to think about, to voice a grievance, to complain, and—of course this seldom happens—to applaud what has been done in the past. The moral and psychological value of such an outlet cannot be estimated. But I won't claim that it's not often a very tiresome ordeal to live through. The seats are hard, people do repeat themselves, the man who thinks he's funny tells the same old jokes, the meeting lasts and lasts and lasts, till we are often worn to a frazzle, as we troop out after governing ourselves. But one result is that there has never been in town anybody who feels, with reason, that he has not had a fair chance to represent his side of any question.

I believe this is as good a place as any to tell you about the officials elected at Town Meeting who run what might be called our Arlington government. Every one of these lives in town. (State and County officials are not elected at Town Meeting.) Some of them—like the Tree Warden and Cemetery Commissioner—work for nothing. Some of them are paid—a little. I can and will tell you what their "salaries" are—all except that of the Road Commissioner. In a mountainous town, plenty of streams go berserk after heavy rains or the melting snows in springtime, and the Road Commissioner is a very important person. He is subject to election every year at Town Meeting and, because his work is visible to everybody's eyes, it is watched with formidable attentiveness by all citizens. But it is hard to report on his pay, because it is set down in the printed, annual Town Report. The item "Labor on Roads" lumps together the pay for his work and that of all the other men who, summer and winter, have plowed snow, filled in mudholes, mended bridges on the "Town Roads." The total cost of labor on roads for which the Town of Arlington is responsible came, last year, to $2,303.10.

Three Selectmen represent what you would probably think of as the mayor. The Chairman of this governing body of three gets $200 a year; the clerk, $125; the third member, $100. The Poormaster (sometimes called the Overseer of the Poor) is paid $100, and earns it, for nowadays every problem connected with a family in financial difficulty we shift to him or her and think no more about it. One per cent of taxes collected pays our Town Treasurer's salary. Last year that came to $850. Three School Directors are very carefully chosen. The young people of an earning-its-living town are about the only resources it has. They take care of the schools for $425 a year, divided between them. Our one police officer has a magnificent, old Norman name of Constable. His salary is $165 a year. There is a "Second Constable" who last year was paid $35. Once a year, the Auditors go over the town books and their work costs the town a dollar an hour. In addition to these paid officials, we elect at annual Town Meeting a Cemetery Commissioner, a Tree Warden, and a Fence Viewer. The total salaries of all Town officials came last year to $1,358.47.

I must break off here to quote something which William Allen White once said about Vermont communal finances. More than twenty years ago he took on the assignment of writing a biography of President Calvin Coolidge, and, knowing nothing about Vermont, came to make us a visit. He had been told that there has been, in the two-century-old life of this State, practically no political corruption. Being an experienced American politician in a big and (so it seems to Vermonters) rich Middle-Western state, he didn't believe this. But afterwards, when he found that this was true, he gave a disillusioned explanation. "There are so few nickels in Vermont," he wrote, "that everybody in the state knows where each one of them is at all times. It's impossible for anyone to lay a hand on one that doesn't belong to him." Perhaps so. At any rate, not one of our town officials has ever helped himself out of our town treasury, since 1764.

Did you notice, I wonder, that a negligible provision is made in our town for police? I never noticed this till we returned from several years in France during the First

World War. We Fishers brought back with us then an elderly French country-woman who had been our much-valued household helper during those war-years in France. On the evening of the day we reached Arlington, she asked casually, "Who are the local police here?"

"Police?" I asked blankly.

She went on, "I ought to know whom to call in case of difficulty."

Blanker than ever, "What kind of difficulty?"

She answered, "For instance, somebody trying to break into the house to steal things."

I explained, "Well, nobody does. There isn't much to steal, and nobody would have to break in, because our doors are never locked."

She exploded like a bomb. "Doors unlocked!! Why, I never could close my eyes at night in a house where the outside doors aren't locked." I was apologetic. "I'm sorry, but I haven't any idea where the keys are. We haven't locked them for—well, never, since we've lived here."

She was pitiably frightened. What could we do? Finally my husband, Mélanie watching him to be sure, nailed shut our outside doors, to give her some peace of mind.

What happened? Nothing dramatic. Arlington is not a dramatic place. A perfectly simple solution followed, as by osmosis. She just lived here a while, and became aware of the moral climate around her. It wasn't long before she thought no more about unlocked front doors.

That's what has happened always, we now perceive. I suppose such an adjustment to the local social climate happens all over the United States. People who come in from outside with quite different notions about human communal relations sometimes like our ways, sometimes dislike them. But if they stay they get used to them. We find that, like everybody else, we take our own ways for granted until someone comments on them. For instance, now, in this attempt to give you some notion of what kind of place my home town is, I can hardly think what to tell you, it is all so familiar to me. What *do* reporters set down in a brief survey of a community? Oh yes, of course, the industrial life carried on there.

Our "industrial life" consists of two sizable factories—with perhaps two hundred odd employees in each one, sometimes a few more, sometimes a few less—and a number of small, very small, family-sized woodworking establishments. One of our two large industries, the Hale chair factory, is now more than a hundred years old. It was begun by an Arlington man, who, like many others long ago, as they do now, "worked in the woods," with his own ax. But Mr. Hale stepped over the boundary line from individual labor to industrialism. Instead of selling the lumber he cut as boards and rafters, he started making it into chairs and tables. Tables and chairs are still made there, very good ones, too. The children and grandchildren of this founding family have now just evaporated into the general American scene. The factory is now being run by a member of an old European furniture-making family, a man who came here during the Hitler terror, and has lived here ever since. He is now married and has a family of young children, Austrian, Czechoslovakian by blood, growing up as Vermonters. Would it interest you to know that, except for an occasional vacation, this factory has never been closed in the hundred years of its life?

Nothing like this in the other "large" factory. Its history reflects the shifts in nineteenth-century American industrial life. From 1850 to 1877 it was a sash-and-blind factory. But it could not hold its own against the enormously bigger sash-factories elsewhere. In dismay, Arlington saw the factory closed and empty. From 1877 to 1909 some metal work was done—car-wheels for railroad use.

But both the raw material and the finished product were heavy. To carry them in and out of a remote mountain town cost too much. That factory closed, too. About 1911 the building came to life once more—refrigerators were made there. Do you, I wonder, young modern as you probably are, know what a refrigerator was? In your vocabulary it might be called a frigidaire kept cold by chunks of ice, old-fashioned frozen water. For a generation, Arlington was once more "stable," as—to look at it now—you'd think it always had been.

An earthquake, a landslide, burst upon the modern world —throwing out of use all over the country hundreds of thousands of iceboxes. A chemically cooled contraption was invented—the frigidaire. Our local factory slowed down, closed its doors. That *was* a dip in the Arlington graph! As by a typhoon, the wage-earning employment of all those people who had worked for a generation in the refrigerator shop was swept away.

For nine long years the building stood idle, looking to us like an unburied corpse. When I tell you that this happened in 1930, you will not need exclamation points from me. Nobody who went through the grim ordeal of the Great Depression will ever forget it.

The East Arlington chair factory did not entirely close. But almost. Fewer and fewer days-work a week, fewer and fewer work-weeks in the year. Our old town might be entirely given up, abandoned. But where in the United States of the long, black passage of our national life could we go? Everywhere the throbbing pulse of the United States industry was stilled. Everywhere the disaster which darkened Arlington life hung like a pall. What could be done? The kind of people who always get panic-struck notions in emergencies were thoroughly panic-struck.

But there are other kinds of people, some here as everywhere. Almost at once, that first bleak spring, an informal get-together meeting was held in our Town Hall for men of the wage-earning age. Anybody could go who wanted to, and some of the women went. I was among them and heard what was said. I shall never forget it. Plainly dressed men who had worked hard all their lives and earned a decent living for their families, and now had no work to do, sat heavily in the old chairs, their faces tense. Their eyes were anxious. But they were not silent. In emergencies, our way of life has been to put our heads together and discuss things. They did this now. The general sense of the meeting, as I heard it, came to something like this: "About a hundred and sixty-six years ago our folks, our ancestors, came up the valley and settled in Arlington. It's the same town. The folks who made a go of it to begin with lived plain but they lived. Nobody has starved here since then. Why should we? We're just as smart as our grandfathers were, and we have lots more machines to help us and lots more know-how about using machinery and lots more is now known about growing food. The land's just the same as it was then, only probably better because it's been cultivated and manured ever since 1764. We needn't go hungry.

"And we needn't freeze. We still know how to cut trees down. Nobody need be cold as long as we own an ax.

"We all have some kind of roofs over our heads. Any house in town is better than the log cabins the first settlers put up. We haven't grown so soft that we can't live plain, too, if we have to."

"If we stick together—"

"Let's go—"

What was settled in this informal get-together and in later ones was a plan: A wide field (wide for Vermont and Arlington) in the bottom of the valley—which had always been used for hay—was to be used for growing food, each family having a plot of it. The initial work of plowing and harrowing was to be done in one big job by modern machines, loaned generously by a family with money who some years before had come here to live. There each man would grow as much food as he could on his plot.

Even in a short Vermont summer you can grow a lot of potatoes, and potatoes are filling. Green vegetables can be canned and every Arlington woman knew how to do this. Vitamin sources, like cabbages, apples, root crops like beets and carrots, can be stored in winter in cellars. And the wild fruit—! The wild strawberries, blueberries, raspberries, blackberries that were put up, the applesauce that was canned—!

It would take too long to tell you in detail how the people of the small, plain community managed to keep their self-respect and to survive when suddenly hurled out of the twentieth century back into pre-industrial life. Here, as elsewhere during the depression, there was no money, so to speak. Well, Arlington people "traded" as they had in the 1800's. A family with a cow, or cows, "sold" their milk for days-work. Owners of wood lots let their neighbors cut firewood, on halves. People who lived in rented houses paid their rent in work. But a large majority of people in town owned their own homes. Not one family was ever put out for non-payment of rent.

That was a savagely rough passage in our community's life, as in our nation everywhere. But what was suffered here was caused by straight material hardships, visible, understandable, to be resisted by effort. Such hardships wound human tissues: but in healthy organisms, scar tissue forms normally over such wounds in the course of time. It was never the paralyzing, numbing, demoralizing situation of the city wage-earner who has lost touch with older ways of surviving. Here in Arlington the situation was not one in which human beings were humiliated by helplessness, it was not one in which individual effort has lost all its meaning.

Those black years did not last too long for our survival, either individually or as a community. For after a while, Hitler, doing as much evil to the world as he could, did us a good service by sending us capital, industrial know-how, and the good will to run the old chair factory along modern lines. And a big New Jersey manufacturing company selected Arlington as the town for setting up a branch of their business, using the old icebox factory building. Once more the shriek of the factory whistle with heartening regularity echoed from the mountain walls of our valley. And it has so echoed ever since.

Perhaps in your ears a factory whistle is a harsh, dissonant note in the orchestra of modern life. If so, you have managed somehow, whether you realize it or not, to live inside a compartment shut off, isolated, water-tight, air-tight, insulated from the pulsing whole of our times. One item in the report I am making to you about what kind of town my home town is, is that Arlington does not live in any such compartment. We are thankful that it does not. You can't understand how life looks to us unless you open your mind to the fact that—poor, small, remote, rural settlement that Arlington is (but not class-segregated)—it is plain to us that, although fewer than a third of us work in factories, we are an organic part of twentieth-century industrial life, as a capillary in the blood is a living part of the body. The tissue in our old cell is fed by new living blood. Our town has not become a museum piece, dusted off every morning by a curator. Our community once more draws its own economic breath. This resumption of regular industrial production did not open doors wide to flowery fields. Not much! But our town was no longer shut in behind bolts and bars. Doors could now be pushed open by individual effort and that lets in air to breathe.

Like everybody else who comes here "to live" (that expression here means "to earn his living"), the newcomers have adjusted themselves to Arlington, and Arlington to them, with few fireworks on either side. I suppose the explanation of this adjustment is that, as in every good bargain, the arrangements suit both sides and are profitable to both.

But I see that I am being—if one may use those academic terms about so casual and discursive a report on our town— too exclusively political and economic. I hope I have brought out the fact that from the beginning of the town, now nearly two hundred years ago, everybody in it has worked for his living. They still do. There never has been any money, in the modern meaning of "money." Only old or sick people have retired from working.

But life is not just work. One of the questions I should answer is, "What do Arlington people do in the hours when they can do what they want to?" I could perhaps take as text for my answer the question often asked of us by people who come in from the United States outside of Vermont, and ask us seriously, "How do you get through the winter up here?"

How do we answer that question? Well, we really don't give any answer. There aren't words to explain to people capable of making a question like that, the variety of social life we have, and how many things we do, without being paid any cash-money for the doing. If I were writing for one of the occasional really "foreign" visitors (from Asia or Europe) who come our way once in a while, note-book in hand, to see what life is in a "typical American village" (are we a "typical" village, I wonder? I suppose we are.), I would here enter on a lengthy, detailed account and explanation of the extraordinary varied community organizations to which we all belong. But you, the reader of these pages, are an American. It would be coals to Newcastle to tell you what meetings of the P.T.A. are, or of the Historical Society, or to describe the Well-Baby Clinic, or the Women's Club meetings, or those of the Altar Guild or the Sodality, or of the Garden Club, or of the Lions Club, the Fish and Game Club, the Grange. You know all about food sales to make money for the running of the Girls Scouts, the Boy Scouts, the High School Student Council—I should have begun the list, I now see, with High School basketball games, always the most exciting, stirringly noisy and well-attended social events of our snowy winters. For here as elsewhere in the United States, the High School is not only an educational institution but the active center of much of what is called social community life, with its competitive games, one-act play contests, and Freshman, Sophomore, Junior and Senior dances. These and weddings are about the only occasions for dressing up which our young people have—and community life would be dry and joyless without recurrent occasions for wearing one's best clothes.

I could go right on with this list—but so could any American except those who live in a big-city background. I leave it to you to add any organizations, social, charitable, religious, the meetings of which you attend, off and on, in the course of your winter life. The same meetings are probably here, too; and are here, as with you, occasions for social contacts with this-and-that group of your fellow-citizens. Often here they are eatings-together of one kind or another—group-sharings of food being, from the cave age on, sure-fire channels of sociability. To know how we in this remote mountain valley "get through the winter," just run over in your mind the occasions on which you take part in the social life of your community and of which you say with some dismay, "I never seem to have a free evening any more."

Yet, of course, Arlington is not entirely and in every detail just a yard cut off the usual American social fabric. For instance, we have no bridge club. Once, some years ago, one was started, but somehow what with rehearsals for amateur theatricals, or (rather our local specialty in this line) group-readings aloud of plays, and meetings of our choral singing groups, and of our active and useful Town Health Association and all the others I'm leaving out from the list, nobody seemed to have time enough for playing bridge, and that group soon stopped functioning.

Our Library was founded in 1806. We think it gets better and more useful all the time as modern life demands better books. But what makes it special is, we think, that its Board of Directors really runs it, *including the choice of books*. There are about twenty-five people on that Board, a ridiculously large number for such a small town. But this means that every variety of reader is represented, young mothers, farmers, industrial workers, retired professors of Latin, country dwellers, people who live in our villages, men, women, Catholic, Protestant, no church. When you have a Board of Directors like that, each one of them knows what the people in his particular circle like to read. And take it from me, no books stand on our shelves which are not read by somebody.

Do you know, I wonder, how the books on the shelves in your own public library were chosen? Perhaps you will say, "By the Trustees and the librarian." But who are the Trustees? My guess is that they are a small number of substantial bankers or merchants who mostly think their business is to see that the library building is kept in good repair. The choice is generally made by your librarian out of the American Library Association and other lists. This variegated group in Arlington meets once a month, and every other month we have a supper meeting, a "covered-dish supper" where everybody brings one item of the communal meal. Twenty to thirty people sit down at the long tables in the two big living rooms of the Community House, talking sociably at the tops of their voices. After the dinner they draw together for a discussion of what books to buy out of our budget, which is, I needn't tell you, not very large. This meeting sounds more like a political caucus than a voting for a selection of books. There are about five thousand books in the Library now, and because the space is very limited, we rigorously weed books in which nobody is interested. Every book which is no longer needed is taken out after so long a time. The stacks are open, anyone can come in (and does), wander around and pick out his own books, taking away several at a time if he likes. There's a children's room (formerly the pantry of the big, old house in my great-grandmother's day) which is brightly painted, with a low table, long and wide, at which the children sit in low chairs, browsing. How we love to see them there!

Have I set down enough, I wonder, so that a reader in Illinois, or New Jersey, or Idaho, will be interested in glimpses into the very ordinary way in which a poor Vermont mountain town (by "poor" I mean with very little extra available cash) manages its communal needs for jobs, food, shelter, and enjoyment?

There is one item inside the school building which we take for granted, but visitors from the outside world do not. On the platform of our school auditorium is Old Glory, standing proudly in its standard, and across the platform from it is the flag of Vermont with its pine tree, and its rather unskillfully drawn cow, the sheaves of grain and the blue mountains in the background.

The Arlington person who is acting as guide calls the attention of the visitor to the two flags as part of the school equipment. We explain casually that they are both part of our patriotic programs. The visitor is apt to comment, "*Two* flags? Don't children get confused? Surely the younger ones can scarcely grasp the idea of *two* loyalties."

When this was first said, it was a new idea to us. We hardly knew how to answer. But now, soberly and sure of fact, we say, "No, American children are used to having two loyalties, one to the state, one to the nation, the union of each of them equally dear, you know, rather like loving both your father and mother. Youngsters take it naturally enough."

We don't mention a third flag, there in that gathering place for the boys and girls of Arlington—the flag of our town. We find plenty of room in everybody's heart for a close, responsible affection to that one, too. But that flag is invisible, and so intimate a part of our daily lives that we don't talk about it.

EIGHTEENTH CENTURY

Uncle Belus Hard
and the Devil

There were no pleasures in my childhood greater than the long, leisurely expeditions taken with Uncle Zed in the phaeton drawn by an elderly roan nag called Dick. Uncle Zed's errands took him near and far, and for every corner of the countryside we visited, there was a story in Uncle Zed's memory. Up near the Baker Bridge in the North District is a grassy bank where he always told me he had seen British prisoners of the War of 1812, soldiers in their red coats, resting on their way south. In Sunderland he always pointed out to me the spot where Ethan Allen stood in a great storm, calling on the lightning to strike him dead if his not being a church-member made him an evil man. At a certain place in the pine-woods, he and his little brother (my grandfather), going on an errand, had met a bear. And, he never failed to say, proudly, "We went on along about our business, too. We didn't give up and run home." When we drove to East Arlington he always looked up at the rocky ridge back of where the Congdon house now stands and said, "Right up there, in those rocks, is where Uncle Belus Hard met the Devil."

"Oh, Uncle Zed, tell me about it again!"

"Well, it was in the old times, just after the Revolution, when lots of folks still believed in witchcraft and magic charms, and put a sprig of St. John's-wort over the churn to make the butter come, and all that sort of goings-on. Over in East Arlington there was a man who said he was in league with the Devil. He could get the Devil to help any man in his work, make his crops grow, keep his cattle well, see that his wife obeyed him—get on in the world twice as fast as he would otherwise.

"Of course Satan didn't do this for nothing. When did he ever? If you wanted him on your side, you went to this agent of his, talked the matter over with him, and paid him a certain sum of money. That was the first thing. Then if he could persuade the Devil to be on your side, you went with the sorcerer, at midnight, in the dark of the moon, up on that ridge of rocks. There you swore that when you died Satan could have your soul in return for his favoring you. You signed this promise with a quill pen dipped in your own blood by the light of a birch-bark torch.

"Then the Devil's agent vanished, leaving you alone, in jet-black darkness. You waited, cold chills going up and down your back, listening for dear life. For a while, not a sound. Then some vague rustlings. And like a gun going off, bang! a great explosion of red fire back of the jagged rock. Flame and smoke poured up. In the midst of it, black and hairy, was a great horned head, a ghastly black face and rolling

« 34 »

white eye-balls. He gave one frightful screech, and disappeared into the blackness. I tell *you,* a man's heart beat fast for a month of Sundays after that night.

"The Devil's agent made a good thing out of this business. Neither he nor his old mother had to do a lick of work. It was as sure as shooting that the Devil took care of *them!* Little by little, in whispers, the news spread around, and some of the simpler farmers on the back roads came in after dark to the sorcerer's house to buy the favor of the Devil.

"Uncle Belus Hard first heard about it when somebody told him his daughter's husband was half thinking about making that bargain, because he wanted to be sure to make a go of a new saw-mill he was setting up. Uncle Belus didn't say a word. But that night he went stubbing on his two canes over to the sorcerer's house and said *he* wanted to sell his soul to the Devil and get prosperous. The sorcerer was astonished, for Uncle Belus was a strict Churchman. But he was quite set up, and said he'd do his best. The bargain was made, just as usual, except that Uncle Belus said he guessed he wouldn't sign the paper or hand over the money till he'd actually seen the Devil. Maybe, he said, the Devil might have a prejudice against him on account of his going to church so much. But the sorcerer said that oh no, the Devil didn't mind that a bit, and that some of his best customers were church-goers, and he'd guarantee the appearance of the Devil.

"So up they went to the rocky ridge, old Uncle Belus leaning on his two heavy canes. The sorcerer disappeared, after whispering that Uncle Belus was not to stir because the air was full of invisible imps.

"Uncle Belus waited. And as he waited he shifted his hold on those two heavy canes till he held them like clubs. There was rustling in the dark, and then BANG!—right in front of him was an explosion, a great red flame flared up and in the midst of it appeared the horrible black creature with long sharp horns, flinging his hairy arms up, and giving a screech enough to raise the hair on a stone image.

"Uncle Belus flung his arms up, too, and he had a heavy cane in each hand. And he had a screech of his own. He'd been a sergeant in the French-and-Indian War, so in spite of being old, he had all the voice there was, when he felt like letting it out. He let it out then, in a sort of Indian war-whoop, shouting, 'If you are the Devil, *stand*! If you are a man, *RUN!*' And he started for the Devil, right through the flames, as if he were leading a charge on a battlefield."

At this point Uncle Zed always stopped to laugh, his long, loud, hearty laugh, as resonant as the ringing old voice with which he imitated Uncle Belus's challenge.

"Well sir," he went on, "the poor gump didn't even stop to catch his breath. He lit out for home as fast as he could leg it, and Uncle Belus after him, yelling like an Iroquois.

"By the time he got back to his own house, he'd lost what little head he ever had (he was only a simpleton anyhow), and when Uncle Belus burst in through the back door stamping and whooping, he found the Devil's right-hand man hiding in bed behind his old mother, the cow-horns sticking up over the top of the sheet. The neighbors came running just in time to see Uncle Belus pull out the black cowhide and throw it in the fireplace."

"Well, I bet there weren't any more souls sold to the Devil around here, after *that*!" I said with a laugh.

Uncle Zed looked at me quizzically, and gathered the reins up over the sleepy old roan. *"What"*ll you bet?" he asked me.

An Eighteenth-century
Gallup Poll

Ethan Allen lived in Sunderland for a while, in early days, and was often in Arlington. One day in 1780 he was standing on our Main Street. A stranger rode into town, got off his horse and asked a bystander where Ethan Allen lived. He was told, "That's Ethan Allen, the tall fellow with the muddy boots, over there on the corner." The stranger went up to Allen and gave him a sealed letter. Then he rode away.

That doesn't sound like much for Arlington people to think about, does it? But we do. Whenever the national or international going gets rough and the road ahead into the future looks dark and uncertain, we think of our roughneck Vermont hero, standing on our plain village street where we go to the post office for our mail. We see him, his rough, bold, weather-worn face grave and anxious, bent over that letter.

He held it in his hand a long time, reading it and rereading it with troubled eyes. Then, so deeply concerned that he didn't nod to the people who said "good morning" as he passed by, he climbed up the hill to Governor Chittenden's house to talk over with him one of the most puzzling, bewildering questions ever faced by conscientious men. *What was the right thing to do?* On the answer to that question hung the future of Vermont. Maybe of much more than Vermont.

Here was something which needed more than reckless bravery, of which our tall, vital frontiersman always had plenty. This was a complicated matter, with all sorts of angles to it, in which the sound good judgment of an older, more thoughtful man was needed.

There he stands, a tall shadow from long ago, to remind us that our generation is not the only one to have hard knots to untie.

Here was the situation which, in the little old frame house on the hill above Arlington, was talked over that day in 1780 by Governor Chittenden and Ethan Allen. The Revolutionary War was going on. Nobody had any idea how long this War for Independence would last, nor which way it would end. The natural sympathies of Vermonters—it goes without saying—were with those who rebelled against the claims of England to force them to live in the way approved by the British Government. It looked to the Green Mountain people exactly like their resistance, year after year, to the claims of the government of the Province of New York to issue orders to them about their way of life. Both sets of rebels were turning their backs on the past and fighting (as they saw it and as we their descendants still see it) for the right to move on into a freer future.

But these naturally warm Vermont sympathies for the American Federation of Colonies (now calling themselves "American States") were blocked by the fact that the American Congress had made it quite clear that Vermont was not wanted in the American Federation of States.

Why?

Because its admission and recognition as a State by the American Congress would mean recognition of the title of its citizens to their own homes and farms. And powerful New York landlords would have none of *that*! They wanted to add those Vermont farms to their already large holdings in the Hudson Valley. Those New York land-owning delegates to Congress were the shrewdest politicians ever! There was mighty little about back-room and committee wire-pulling which those politically astute New York delegates in Philadelphia didn't know. So far, they had been able to block any action by Congress recognizing Vermont as a State.

On the other hand, Congress did not wish wholly to turn its back on Vermont, for the Green Mountain region was geographically valuable in the American fight for Independence. Through those valleys and especially over Vermont waterways, the British forces in Canada could pour down a terrible flank attack.

So Vermonters were left dangling. On their northern boundary were the British armed forces, massed ready for a military invasion which would sweep over their land. On their southern boundary were the threatening landlords, lawyers and politicians, of the Province of New York. To advance their own financial interests these politicians constantly described Vermonters to the leaders of Congress as a formless rabble of lawless, brutal mountaineers. Vermont, without any representation in Congress, had nobody to speak for them to

refute this charge. Our forefathers saw clearly that their independence as citizens of a poor, small "independent republic"
was in danger of its life. They had plenty of courage but,
realistically considered, they had very few material resources
for defending themselves against the two great powerful forces
threatening them on both sides. Those ancestors of ours were
holding out, yes, but they were desperately tired of walking a
political tightrope over disaster.

After the arrival of that momentous letter in Arlington,
months followed of hesitation and discussion between the
representatives of the British Government and Vermont.
For several generations, little or nothing came out in public
about that fateful discussion, but from opened-up government
archives, we now know exactly what they were talking about
—the letter contained an official proposition from Sir Henry
Clinton, Commander of the British armed forces in America,
saying that the British were prepared to make a separate peace
with Vermont. The mother-country invited Vermonters to go
on being what they had been from their birth, self-respecting
British subjects, Colonists of England with recognized political
rights, just as they always had had, back in the Connecticut
from which they had come, with just such freehold titles to
their farms as Connecticut people had always enjoyed under
British rule. Why go on, vainly asking to be recognized as one
of the new States, and admitted to the American Congress?
It was perfectly evident that they were not wanted.

The details were known only to leaders on both sides. But
rumors flew up and down Vermont.

This kind of "secret diplomacy" was not at all to the taste
of Ethan Allen who never liked anything secret. After a while
he wrote bluntly to the President of the American Congress,

"I do not hesitate to say I am fully grounded in opinion that Vermont has an indubitable right to agree on terms of cessation of hostilities with Great Britain provided that the United States persist in rejecting her application for union with them."

It must be remembered that Vermonters of that period were not (as we are apt to think) "American citizens" faced with the question of whether to turn against "their" country. The citizenship which they had inherited was British. The very conception of being "an American" was brand-new. The government of England offered them a continuation of the old citizenship which, they knew from experience in Connecticut and Massachusetts, had allowed their fathers to set up a society with free schools, local self-government, honest courts and equal political rights for all men. No such possibilities were offered to them by the Hudson Valley landlords—quite the contrary.

As to what Vermonters of that year felt about this proposition, we have unusually full information. General Haldimand, then Commandant in Canada, sent a capable secret agent into the Vermont countryside to find out the sentiments of the Green Mountain people—a sort of eighteenth-century Gallup Poll. After intensive field observation, going from one settlement to another, talking with all sorts of people, the agent returned to Canada. The evidence he had collected was carefully sifted and weighed. These were the findings: among the leading men of Vermont, about a third, disheartened by the refusal of the Philadelphia Congress, were inclined towards the British proposition. Of the leaders, another third were aggressively anti-British. The last third were bewildered and undecided.

But, the British agent's report went on, as for the "common

people," the ordinary Vermonters, they were ready to (I quote) "accept any government *except* that of New York."

Before any public declaration could be made, everything was changed by the news of Cornwallis's surrender at Yorktown in October, 1781. The British in Canada withdrew rapidly from their side of the negotiations and the Vermonters from theirs. That momentous question never needed to be answered.

Ethan Allen pushed the letter back in the drawer of his desk. That was that.

The Chittenden Way
of Life

The first governor of Vermont lived in Arlington, up near the railroad station where the new Masonic building stands. A bronze memorial tablet on that slope commemorates the presence here of the Chittendens.

But no homely stories of everyday life ever get put into bronze. It costs too much. So, from the inscription on this tablet, you would never guess what kind of people the Chittendens were. They were perfectly in accord with the general Vermont idea that people who don't work with their hands and muscles have no call to look down on those who do.

One of the favorite stories still told about them in Arlington is of a well-dressed traveler, who had business with Governor Chittenden, riding up from the South and looking for somebody to ask about the whereabouts of the Chittenden home. When he drew near to Arlington, the narrow dirt road was completely blocked by a big hay wagon. The driver, who sat high up on it driving the two horses, was an old fellow with grizzled hair and plain farmer's clothes. The stranger, who wore a three-cornered hat and a wide-skirted bright blue coat with lace ruffles and gold buttons, called out to him: "Can you tell me where His Excellency Governor Chittenden lives?"

The old farmer turned his head and called back: "I'm going there. Follow me."

The elegant stranger assumed that the old fellow in the workingman's smock-frock was one of the servants employed at the gubernatorial mansion; for in the American colonies of the eighteenth century the governors lived in "a style befitting their rank," as the saying used to run. For the same reason, dressed handsomely, too, with silk coats and velvet breeches, silk stockings, and silver buckles on well-polished shoes.

The hay wagon crawled slowly around many turns in the narrow road. The gentleman rider jogged impatiently behind it. Finally they arrived at a plain, small, farmer's house. Across the road was a barn and barnyard. And here the hay wagon turned in.

The astonished rider followed. The hay wagon halted, the old farmer slid down to the ground, gave the reins to a waiting boy, turned to the man in fine broadcloth, dusted off his hands, and said pleasantly, "I'm Governor Chittenden. What can I do for you?"

Another story is about Mrs. Chittenden. Some fine city folks had come up from Massachusetts to see her husband about business. These visitors from a state where the governor never appeared without a powdered wig and never went out except in a coach were surprised to see Mrs. Chittenden herself, aproned from neck to hem, getting the dinner, bustling to and from the kitchen into the dining room where a long table was spread.

But they were even more surprised when the wife of the chief executive of Vermont stepped to the door and rang the big bell which, she explained, was to call in the men working in the hayfield.

Seeing the gentlemen look surprised, she said mildly, with the dry Vermont, ironic turn which we treasure, "I know, it must seem odd to you that we eat at the same table with the haymakers. Of course I realize they've been out in the hot sun all the morning, while we have been here, comfortable, in the house. By rights, they should eat first and we should wait our turn. But I thought since you were company, they wouldn't mind having us all eat together."

Remember Baker

In East Arlington, on the road leading up to the Kelly Stand, is a big, rough stone monument. On it is a bronze tablet with the date of Remember Baker's birth and death, and the statement that he was a leader in the Vermont struggle not to live under the government of the Province of New York. Nothing in these facts gives any idea of the exciting night in 1772 when the New York sheriff came up with his posse to East Arlington to arrest Remember Baker and take him away to the Albany jail.

The bronze tablet would need to be as big as the boulder itself, if on it were set down, even in the fewest possible words, the exciting events which led up to that midnight raid, for they began centuries before the sleigh of the York State sheriff drove into East Arlington and halted menacingly before the door of Remember Baker's home.

What was at stake was one of the biggest questions of human history—whether ordinary men should own the land they cultivated, or should pay rent for their fields to a landlord who never worked himself, but had the legal right not only to get an income from another's labor, but also to put the farmer out of the house he and his family lived in, and off the fields which he had plowed and harrowed and seeded. The just-beginning settlements in the Green Mountains offered to their people the right to own in permanent tenure the land they worked, the right to vote as freely as people with more money, the right to have a system of free public schools for their children, the right to courts of law where a poor man without influential connections had as fair a chance at justice as anybody else.

The eighteenth-century Province of New York offered no such living conditions. Great areas of the good farming lands along the Hudson were owned by a few landlords, trying to reproduce the "gentry and working people" way of life, then existing in the farming districts of England. The men who did the work on the land were tenant-farmers who could not renew their leases unless the proprietor approved of the way they voted—if indeed they were allowed to vote at all. The ruling officials did not wish the children of farmers to go to school because (they said so themselves in black and white) education would lessen the "spirit of subordination," which they valued in poor people. Politically there was mighty little local self-government which, like free public schools, was disliked and limited as much as possible by the government of the Province. The Green Mountain settlers, you see, insisted on creating a way of life actively detested by those in power in the Province of New York.

And, those two opposing ways of life lay very close to each

other, so short a distance between them that it didn't take long for a sleigh to be driven from one to the other. These were the two opponents in a long, long fight, who suddenly, when that sleigh came gliding in over the snow to East Arlington, stepped forward close enough to each other to come to blows.

That midnight skirmish, although big enough for us to commemorate by a monument with a bronze tablet, is no more than the tiniest paragraph in the age-old story of a struggle which, even now in 1955, is encircling the globe. All over the Orient, people are hoping and praying for just what those eighteenth-century Vermont farmers stood ready to fight for.

Those Persian peasants, the skeleton-thin tenant-farmers of India reaching out their hands eagerly for a piece of Mother Earth on which they may raise food to be eaten by the people who need it, not to put money into the already full pockets of absentee landlords—they are brothers of our Remember Baker, and his neighbors, our great-grandfathers. If anybody can understand the Asian revolt from landlordism, we Vermonters can.

One of the bizarre elements in the New York-Vermont fight between two contrasting ways of life was that it was not one which could be settled by shooting. It was a long-drawn-out battle of wits—the brains of farmers pitted against the professionally skilled lawyers of the Hudson Valley landlords. Every Vermonter of that time understood that there must be, on our side, no violence. For if our ancestors shed any New York blood, the sharp landlord clan could represent to the British Government that the Green Mountain folks were lawless, murderous gangsters, and call on the British Army for protection. Farmers, their cabins scattered through the forests, armed only with squirrel guns, could not hope to stand against the finely equipped professional soldiers of an Empire.

In this chess game there was a move to which the landlord-gentry hoped the Vermont farmer could be forced—to have the matter at issue brought into the New York courts. If this could be arranged, everybody knew what would happen, for from jailor to judge, from lawyer to jury, the eighteenth-century courts of the Province of New York were filled with partisans of landlordism. If the trial was between a farmer who wanted to own the land he cultivated and a landlord who wanted rent, it was always settled in favor of the landlord.

Only five or six years before that night of the twenty-first of March, 1772, when the New York sheriff's sleigh appeared in East Arlington, dozens of tenant-farmers in the Hudson Valley had been put into prison, had been fined, had been set in pillories—punished for resisting arrest when the sheriff called on them to surrender. And one fine, upright, hard-working, kind-hearted farmer had been condemned to horrible torture and death for being their leader.

Remember Baker was such a leader.

So far, the tale has been set down as documents in official records show the facts to have been. It was told in another way by the people who were old folks when those of my generation were young.

"Now, children," they used to say, "right up this road came the New York State armed officials in the black of night to take Baker to jail. They got him down, and dragged him out into the sleigh. Then they raced away towards Albany, whipping their horses to top speed to get our Vermonter into the Province where any court would be on their side. And out from their low-ceilinged homes, just like our homes now—all they had in the world—swarmed our great-grandfathers to rescue Baker.

"Don't forget that to resist an officer of the New York law was then a life-and-death matter. Remember Baker's chances for life were slim if he could be carried off to be tried in the law courts of the New York Province where rich landowners called the tune.

"Two of Baker's neighbors tried instantly to stop the sheriff's sleigh. Two ordinary men against an armed posse with guns and bayonets. Baker was wounded in the fracas. One of those neighbors was seized, taken prisoner and carried along towards Albany. The other escaped, gave the alarm, and a messenger was sent off at top speed, by a short cut, to collect help from men farther down the line towards Bennington. Like Paul Revere, that long-ago East Arlington neighbor of ours raced through the blackness down our Valley, and like the men of Concord and Lexington, the men of Shaftsbury and Bennington rallied and came galloping up the main road to cut off the New York party. They were met—all this still in pitch-black darkness—by Arlington and Sunderland men urging their horses to help in the rescue.

"Keep in mind, children, that all those then-young ancestors of yours knew that they were risking their necks. Not one of them could be sure that he would ever come home. And here's something for us all to remember. *Not one of them knew beforehand that the others would turn out.* The safe thing to do was to stay right at home in bed behind closed doors under their own roofs. Such an easy thing to do! But if they had taken that easy way, we wouldn't be here now with roofs of our own over our heads.

"Well, they didn't. Yet they had not one minute to think it over, to call a meeting, to encourage one another, to listen to a speech by a leader. Nobody told them what to do. Each man was his own leader and knew what to do.

"Look back at them, that cold winter night, leaping out of their warm beds, snatching up their outdoor clothes, shouting to their sons to hurry out to the barn and saddle the horse. They swung themselves up and pelted down the road after the dangerously powerful officer of the law who was carrying off, perhaps to his death, a man who believed as they did, that it should be possible for an American to own the land he plowed.

"Look back through two centuries at those young fathers of families defending their homes—our homes now. Can't you see them, black against the snow, reining in when they overtook the sheriff's sleigh, halting the New York horses, shouting, scuffling, lifting the bleeding Baker to the saddle on a Vermont horse, and galloping home through the night, their hearts bright with pride in their courage...."

Our young hearts, too, were bright with that pride.

EARLY NINETEENTH CENTURY

All Right Is Good Enough
for a Chicken House....

In a slowly changing community like Arlington, an especial association deepens, one generation after another, around a geographical spot, because the story is not hustled out of the way by later ones. Along one of our valley roads, there are still some rough, grassed-over, stony marks of ruts which indicate the route taken, a century and a half ago, by a short, steep, side lane which led up to a plateau. This shelf of level ground is now covered with trees. Early in the nineteenth century several houses stood there. They had long been abandoned when I was a little girl, seventy-five years or so ago. Not a sign of human homes was left save a few rose-colored old bricks, tumbled in piles amidst brambles and saplings. But when, my feet swinging high above the floor of the buckboard or low phaeton, which were the only light vehicles of my youth, a great-uncle or great-aunt and I passed the foot of this short side road, the older person glanced up at where the hamlet had stood, and told me again the story of the Jedidiah Searles who had lived there.

Most of the old-time stories of human life here are quite complete, with a beginning, a middle and an end. But this story ended in mystery—until recently. Here was the tale as I heard it long ago: The Searles house had been built there in the late eighteenth century, and had sheltered a normal, comfortable family life from about 1780 to—perhaps the 1830's. For fifty years or so, life had run along in it, the older people growing infirm, and dying, young people taking over, marrying and having children. But all at once—abruptly and mysteriously—this living thread had broken off. Of the Searles family who had built the house, Jedidiah was the last one to live in it. And he had not grown old there, had not died under its roof. The river of his life had plunged suddenly under ground and vanished. Through what inner catacylsm, no one knew.

Yet, so my elders always told me, there had never been anything strange about him. He had been just like anybody else, a strong, hearty farmer and lumberman, he had married a nice wife, a girl from the near-by town of Sunderland, I think, and had had two strong, healthy sons, who were perhaps ten and twelve years old at the time Jedidiah vanished.

The valley road from which we could look up at the little mountain shelf, and catch a glimpse, faintly pink, of old bricks tumbled among the trees, was one of the so-called "main" roads which led south along our valley to Albany in York State, and from there to the West. At first, "the West" meant anything beyond Albany. And then it meant Ohio, then it meant Indiana and Illinois. Finally, Iowa, where, in early days, many of our Vermont families settled. The wagon

trains of westward-bound immigrants encountered deep mudholes in the Vermont mountain roads of the early nineteenth
century. All westward-bound travelers expected as a matter of
course to get mired in one mudhole after another. Arlington,
first settled in 1764, had, by the early 1800's, houses fairly
close to each other along the road. The principle of human
solidarity, always respected in primitive living conditions,
made it a duty for decent Vermonters to help emigrant wagons
out of the mudholes nearest their houses, till they could pro-
ceed, slowly and joltingly, on toward the West.

From the Searles house on its slight eminence above the
road, it was easy to look down and follow the fortunes both
of the local and westward-bound travel along it. When the
wheels of a wagon sank into a mudhole, the Searles man who
saw it left his work and stepped down the lane to help out.
Jedidiah had often done this. All Vermont farmers did.

Late one afternoon, about 1820, in autumn, the season when
here in our valley the days shorten and twilight comes early,
Jedidiah was splitting firewood out in front of his house,
overlooking the main road. This chore is easier than many of
the old-time farm tasks, and so was often put off towards the
end of the day because it could be readily stopped whenever
the call to supper came.

He was splitting sticks of oak, bringing his ax up over his
head and letting it fall with the practiced use of gravity to
add power to the blow of the blade. A skillful chopper of
those days (when they began splitting wood at about ten years
of age), by "letting his ax fall" as the phrase ran, could work
for hours on end without being tired. But a boy, just learning
how to chop, and who did it all by main force and awkward-
ness, was worn out in twenty minutes. Oak makes a loud

crack when it splits, and an upraised ax gives out a flash of bright steel even in gathering twilight. The crack of the oak was so heard and the flash was thus seen by a family in a covered wagon down on the main road.

Their back wheels had sunk into one of the bottomless pits of mud. The man of the family came up the little slope to the Searles house, and asked the chopper to help them out. One more time Jedidiah swung his ax up over his head and let it fall, this time not on a stick of firewood, but on the chopping block, from which, ten or fifteen minutes later, he could pull it out when he returned from his neighborly offices.

But he never returned. From that moment, nothing was seen or heard of him.

Darkness fell quickly. His wife had been getting supper in the kitchen in the back of the house. The ringing blows of the ax reached her faintly, through the sputter of frying pork. She did not notice when they stopped. One of her two boys had a sore throat. She was thinking about him, in bed in the little room next to the kitchen. When the old clock struck, she glanced up at it and saw that suppertime had passed and her husband had not come in. She stepped to the kitchen door and called out into the darkness. From her husband, no answer. The older son, the twelve-year-old one, came in from the barn, the milk pail swinging from his hand.

"Where's your father?" she asked the boy casually.

"He was out in front splitting wood. And then some covered-wagon folks got stuck in the mudhole and came up to ask him to help out. He can't be far."

The mother and the big boy called loudly.

No answer. No sound.

The boy set down his pail of milk and went around to the

front of the house. Coming back, he reported, "His ax is still struck into the chopping block just as he left it. He can't be far."

They looked around them blankly. It was black night now, there was no sound.

Over the woodshed roof hung a bell, such as was often used in scattered settlements to call home the men to meals. Jedidiah's wife set it loudly clanging and went back to her sick child and her frying pork.

But Jedidiah did not appear.

Wondering, and now a little uneasy, she and the older son went down the slope together carrying a lantern. By the dim light of the candle in the lantern, they could see the mudhole, the marks of the emigrant wagon still clear. Beyond the hole, the tracks of the wheels showed the emigrant's wagon had gone on down the valley.

She was not a timid woman, not given to fears. Her first thought was that perhaps some neighbors had called her husband in to help with a sick cow, or—she had a new idea—he had some chore to do in the little barn out back, and did not know they were looking for him. She and the boy went all through the barn. Then—perhaps he might be in the house! Hurrying now and alarmed, they ran through the tiny dwelling shouting and calling. No voice answered.

Fearing to leave the sick child alone, she sent the boy to the nearest neighbor's house to know if they had seen anything of Jedidiah. He ran back in a moment, looking scared. "No, they say they haven't seen him at all."

Jedidiah's wife never had any more news of him. He had vanished. She never saw him again. In a perfectly peaceful settlement, with houses and neighbors all around him, close to his own home, a man had disappeared as if the earth had swallowed him.

It was then too dark to send out a searching party. There was nothing his wife could do that night. By early dawn, the neighbors gathered together a little group of men and boys on horseback, and went down the road. But there were several turnings and crossroads, and they didn't know which one to take. Nor could anyone in the houses they passed give them a clue. The wagon had evidently passed along after dark had fallen. None of the neighbors along the way had seen it.

There was no trace. There never was any trace.

But, of course, human imaginations are always active when presented with a mystery. Any number of possible explanations were made up. Here was one: That the party of people in the covered wagon had not been decent, harmless travelers like most of those who passed along, but a gang of murderers or thieves, who had attacked Jedidiah from behind, killed him and carried his body along with them. That was like the blood-and-thunder, horror stories in fashion at that time which was at the height of the Romantic school. Nobody in the plain, Vermont settlement had ever heard of such a thing happening out of a book. But this guess came to be discussed a great many times over hearth fires in the little houses along Vermont roads. Why would anybody want to kill him? He hadn't a cent with him. He hadn't even his ax. Nothing but his pocket-knife. Plainly dressed in homespun with deerskin pants, there was nothing on him which would arouse the envy of anybody.

Then, of course, the people who always want to connect sex with any violent event thought that he had perhaps fallen in love with a girl of the emigrant family and gone along with them for that reason. But Jedidiah had been a notably quiet man, never had seemed to notice any woman except the girl he married, and by the time he got down there to the main road it had been so dark that, with the best will in the world, no girl could have seen enough of him or he of any girl for a sudden flame of passion such as was, then as always, put into sensational books.

Another guess was made. He had always seemed on good terms with his wife, but perhaps they had quarreled, and he had been thinking of leaving her. But the social atmosphere of a small settlement, where everybody knows everybody else, is transparent. No such long-continued, family dissension would have been possible without the kinsmen and neighbors all around them knowing something about it. Still, as his two sons grew up, this was the idea which persisted longest in their minds and in neighborhood talk. It really seemed the only possible one. Their father and mother must have quarreled —what else could have been the reason?

For the boys did grow up. Their mother was a vital, energetic woman. She managed the farm, saw to it that the boys had as much education as was available then for anybody, by which they profited, both of them being normally bright. They worked hard and so did she, and the years of their adolescence passed quickly.

As they came to manhood, the mystery of their father's disappearance grew dim in their memories, but took a larger place in their minds. Of course, they thought often of what anybody would have thought of—putting a straight question to their mother. One day, when they were young men grown, they did ask her. She recognized their right and did her best to answer openly. "We always got along all right, as far as I knew," she said. "He was an awfully quiet man. Never said much. But lots of men don't say much. What he did was—all right."

She realized from their expression that she was not giving them satisfaction. So she went on, "He was a good provider, always went to church, never looked at another woman." She hesitated, her honest eyes wide-open to her sons' enquiry. "He never thought of going West himself," she went on, "anyhow he never said a word about it. If he had wanted to, I'd have been willing to go."

She drew a long breath, and trying to open more widely a door which had always been kept closed, she said, "I'd have done anything he wanted to. If he had spoken about it."

The young men had lived closely with their mother for years. Nothing in her could have been hidden from them. They knew her to be honest to her last fiber. They fell silent. She, too, was silent.

Then she leaned forward and said earnestly, "You know, boys, I'd tell you if I knew anything more."

Yes, they did know this. At the very end of their talk, their mother added, hesitatingly, "Sometimes I thought—" but she did not finish that sentence. She tried again, "Once I wanted to—" but she could not find the right words. She only said once more, "We always got along all right."

They did not know how to ask the questions which might have helped her find the words.

More years went by. Her sons grew up, married, good marriages in the real meaning of the word, as well as materially. They moved on to other farms. In those days, there was plenty of land, which cost little to buy, more favorable for farming than the old Searles place which, in very early days, had been placed on the only flat ledge of a rough and hilly homestead. After they had gone to homes of their own, their mother lived on in the old house alone for a while. When she grew old, she lived first with one son and then with the other. Then her time came, and she died. No word had ever come from her missing husband.

The old house stood like many another farm home, abandoned for a better situation by the younger generation. At first it looked like itself—from a distance. But it was not long before, even as you passed on the main road below it and looked up at it, it looked as abandoned homes do, like an unburied corpse. Older people passing along looked up, remembered the strange mystery of the disappearance of its first owner and, if they had a child along with them, told the story. I was one of those children. I came to know, as children do know about the reflexes of their elders, that as soon as we turned a certain corner in the valley road, the great-uncle or great-aunt with me would look up, see a heap of tumbled brick and tell me the story. Often they ended, "Sometimes it seems to me I can hear his ax-strokes, still ringing as they did the day he stepped away from his home. He only went a few feet, but he vanished as if he'd stepped over the edge of the world. Whatever in the world happened, do you suppose?"

But then they died. And I began to pass from being entirely grown up to being one of the older generation myself. I, too, as I made the familiar turn in the highway on horseback or in a light wagon, looked up, caught a glimpse of pinkish bricks showing through the weeds and saplings which surrounded the house and sometimes, stopping my horse, listened for the ghostly echo of that long-ago ax ringing out over the valley. I often had a child with me, as older-generation people do. And I went on telling them the story as it had been told to me, long after the time when I realized they had come to know it as well as I had. As we approached that special turn in the road, I could feel them thinking, resignedly, "Now Mother (or Aunt Dorothy) is going to tell us the story about the Searles man who disappeared from his home up there, and how, if she listens, she can hear his ax splitting wood." But I knew that they never heard the ax. And I knew they were bored with the story, so after a while I stopped telling it.

I never knew his sons, because they were gone before I grew up, old and in their graves, and his grandchildren were scattered all over the valley. Since most of them happened to be girls, married into other families, the very name Searles vanished as utterly as the old brick house. Brambles and old sprawling sumac bushes and trashy popple trees hid the dimly pink rubble of the bricks. The sonorous ring of the ax-strokes became echoes, even in my ears, and then faded into silence.

I thought I had forgotten the story, so many years had gone by since I heard it, or had told it. But does one ever forget a story which is part of real life?

And then I heard the end of it. It was at a "covered-dish supper" at one of our valley churches. I won't stop to tell you now what a covered-dish supper is—though I'm pretty sure you don't know that it is a sort of communal dinner party arranged by everybody for everybody in one of our social groups. As I went into the basement of the church where the tables were set, I saw a good many familiar faces among the older people. But right across the table from me, when I sat down, was a young woman whose face was entirely strange to me—and I mean that not only did I not recognize her individually, but that she didn't, in our valley phrase, "look like anybody." By that we mean anybody we have known among our neighbors. It's rather unusual to see anybody in our valley whose face suggests to older people no family association.

I did know her neighbor, who now leaned over and introduced her, "Let me make you acquainted with Jane Eldridge. She's going to teach school here this winter, and she's quite interested because she said her folks used to tell her about a great-great-grandfather of hers, who, they thought, had lived here."

I knew from long familiarity with the conversational gambits in use around here what was the proper thing for me to say, so I asked, "What was his name?"

Was I astonished when the girl said hesitatingly, "I think the name was Searles."

I laid down my knife and fork and, leaning across the table, inquired quickly, "Was it by any chance Jedidiah Searles?"

The girl from Iowa was as surprised as I. "Why, yes, it was! However did you know?"

I tried to do a sum in my head but gave it up and asked, "How did you ever hear about him? He must have been dead almost a century before you were born."

"Oh goodness yes, I never saw him. It was my grandmother who used to tell me a story about him. She was very old when I heard her talk about it."

"Was it," I enquired, "anything about how he happened to leave Vermont?"

The pretty Iowa girl was astonished again. "Why, yes, it was," she cried. "How did you know?" She went on, "I remember she used to wind up her story with a saying that sounded like a proverb somehow. Maybe it's an old Vermont proverb."

I began to tell her something about how I happened to know, but the loud cheerful gabble of neighborly chatter around us rose to the noisiness which is always taken as a sign that people are enjoying themselves at a party, and she could not hear me. So I leaned across the table and shouted briefly, "Come to see me sometime. I used to hear a story about your great-great-grandfather."

She did come to see me a week or so after this, fresh and twentieth centuryish in up-to-the-minute clothes and hair-do. And, rather to my surprise, she remembered the story her grandmother had told her as well as I remembered the local tales passed along by my older generation. Her grandmother, it turned out, had been a granddaughter of the Searles man whose ghostly ax-strokes had so long echoed in that corner of our valley.

She told the story as everybody does tell a story, with breaks and questions, and pauses for digressions, but I'll set down only that part of it which gave the answer—such an astonishing answer—to the question which Jedidiah Searles' neighbors had so long asked themselves about his disappearance.

"Grandmother said that her grandfather—he was Jedidiah Searles—lived to be very old, outlived his wife and came to live with his son who was my great-grandfather, of course. He became very deaf in his old age, so that my grandmother, who was a little girl then, had it as one of her household tasks to stand by him when he had visitors, which happened seldom, and shout their questions in his ear, as she was the only one of the family who could make him hear.

"One day, two strangers came to call at the house to ask if they could speak to old Mr. Searles. She said they were nice-looking, quiet, farmerlike men, who said they had come all the way from Vermont to ask him a question.

"She went in to stand by the old man's chair to pass the question along in the piercing treble which she had learned to pitch so that it penetrated his deafness. Since she had to repeat everything they said, she remembered pretty well what that conversation had been. The question they wanted to ask was, What had made him leave his Vermont family and vanish? Had he had a quarrel with his wife perhaps? His wife, they explained, had been their mother.

"The little girl was astonished by this odd inquiry, but her grandfather was then too old to be astonished by anything any more. He answered readily enough, No, he hadn't had any quarrel with his wife. She was all right. They always got along all right. Looking back with his faded old eyes to his youth, he went on that he hadn't ever meant to go away when he had stepped down the lane to help the emigrants out of the mudhole. The idea of leaving Vermont had never crossed his mind. No, he really couldn't tell exactly how it did happen. As near as he remembered, the emigrants had asked him if there were other mudholes on the road, and he had said, yes, there were and he knew all about them. So they asked him to go along with them for a little way to help them keep out of the bad places. There was room enough on the front seat of their wagon for him to ride along, holding their little boy on his lap.

"They talked as they rode, and the emigrants got to telling about their plans to settle on new, rich land out West. At first, he hadn't been especially interested. He liked his Vermont home all right. But they kept on going so late that it was pretty dark when they stopped. He hadn't brought any lantern with him, and they didn't have one. The man and his wife slept out on the ground, nights, when it wasn't too cold, with blankets, their little boy between them. They found a couple of extra blankets to loan him for the night. And he slept there, too.

"When he woke up in the morning they were farther along

the road than he'd ever been since he was a boy, he said. It interested him sort of. He thought he'd go along with them for a while longer. And then—he closed his eyes for a moment, as if to try to remember something blurred by the passage of time—what had happened? Oh yes, they had come up with three other wagons going West—one of them stuck fast in the mud. After the mired wagon had been pried loose, the first family had told the others that he knew where the mudholes in the road were. So he went along with them. There were four wagons by that time. A regular little procession. He hadn't meant, not really, to keep on going, but there sort of seemed to be something to do always to help out with one or another of the emigrant wagons. First thing he knew, they got clear down to Troy on the Hudson. There wasn't any way of sending word back to his folks—there was no regular mail in those days—and one of the emigrating families said, Why didn't he go along with them and maybe he could stake out a claim for a good farm out West somewhere and bring his family on.

"So he decided to do just that and went along one day after another. All sorts of things happened, and it took a long while. When they got out to Ohio, well, he didn't know just how it did happen, but somehow he settled down there. No special reason. He didn't hardly realize he was settling there. How could he ever get back to Vermont, all that way, on foot, and without any money or any tools? By that time, he had been gone quite a while—he couldn't remember how long. Maybe they'd forgotten about him back there in Vermont. Then the daughter of a family he was living with wanted to marry him, so he did. Some kind of doings about that—he couldn't rightly remember. They had some children, he set up a little store on one corner of his farm. Always did pretty well on it, too."

You can perhaps imagine that I listened to this life story with incredulous astonishment. The pretty, lively young girl from Iowa found it as dull as I did, but she had no reason, as I had, for a special marveling at its dullness. I imagine it sounded like all grandfather's tales to her. It took a good deal of questioning on my part to draw out from her memory more of what her grandmother had told her so long ago. "It wasn't much of a story," she said. "Nothing much had ever happened. And it was so long ago." It came out that her grandmother had remembered that the two middle-aged Vermont sons had said something to her great-great-grandfather about the ending of his second marriage, with the Ohio farmer's daughter. This second wife (if you could call her a wife, and I suppose she was) had in the very last years of their marriage done a strange thing. After the children were grown up and in homes of their own, she and her husband were left by themselves in the little Ohio farmhouse. As far as anybody knew, they seemed to be getting along all right, but after only two months, the old wife had left her husband to live with one of the married children. Nor would she ever go back to him. When her astonished children questioned her about this, she had no reason to give. She merely said, "No, we never quarreled. He's been all right. He's been a good provider." But when pressed she added one phrase so odd a comment on the strange turn her life had taken that the grandmother who had been the little girl of those days had never forgotten it. She told them once, the impatience of her accent coming down all the years, "No, I *won't* go back and live with your father! No, I—don't try to make me! He's always acted

« 69 »

all right by me. But—" And finally, *"There just ain't any point in our living together."*

The two Vermont farmers asked their old father if he knew any reason for her leaving him. At this he fell into a long silence, seeming to forget almost that they were there. Then, wonderingly, "No sir, I never did understand why she went away that way. No, I never quarreled with her. We lived together all right." It was the phrase he had used about his Vermont wife.

The old man was tired by this time, sagging low in his chair, his head hanging. It is probable that the two Vermonters, even more surprised than I was, were not any more adept at asking questions now than they had been when they had questioned their mother. Nor did they know exactly how to get themselves out of the room. They sat on in a blank silence, their big farmer's hands on their knees.

Suddenly the old man lifted his head, looked at the two sons he had not seen since they were little boys, and said with an odd troubled intonation one phrase, which the little girl shouting in his ear had never been able to forget. "He said it sort of queer," she told her modern granddaughter, who was passing it along to me. "He said—it sounded as if it had just come into his mind and as if he'd never thought of it before. He said, 'Maybe I never paid enough attention to being married.'"

So that was all! The let-down was one of the most complete astonishments I have ever had. I could make nothing out of it. *No* ending! No story! How flat! "A zero with the rim off," as the old folk-phrase runs.

The brisk, rosy young woman from Iowa had found it as flat as I did. She now glanced surreptitiously at her wristwatch. I stirred, "But it seems as though I remember, when we spoke about this at the covered-dish supper, that you said something about a kind of proverb your grandmother used to quote when she told you." She perceived, with evident relief, that it was now socially all right for her to go, and stood up to slip her coat on. "Well, I don't know that it was what you'd really call a proverb," she said, glancing appraisingly at herself in the mirror across the room. "I never heard anybody but Grandmother use it. Maybe she made it up." I rummaged in the last corner of what seemed like an empty box, "Do you remember what it was?" I asked her.

"Oh yes, I remember her saying it ever so many times. We got tired of hearing her. Every time anybody mentioned a husband and wife who weren't getting on very well together, we knew she'd bring it out. 'I guess all right is good enough to build a chicken house out of. *Not a marriage!*'"

That box, after all, had not been empty.

Lawyer Harmon

In early days, long, long before automobiles were thought of, a Mr. Canfield lived in a big white house on the southeast corner of Main Street, where you turn up-hill to go to East Arlington. At that time, there were so many Canfields in Arlington that, to make sure which one was being spoken of, the habit was to use his first name, with some descriptive adjective, such as "Mr. Frank," "Dr. Eli," "Water-Street Charlie." This Canfield was called "Lawyer Harmon." He was a success in his profession, especially in court trials, because he had a fine strong voice and could roar bullyingly at the jury in the way that was admired in the early nineteenth century.

One morning, a century or so ago, he planned to go to Bennington, our shire-town, where he was to conduct a trial, in the County Court-House. (This story is told in two ways: one, that he went by the stagecoach; the other, that he took the train, the very year the newly built railroad began to operate. As I usually heard it, it was of something happening years before the railroad was built.) The stagecoach had just started south, Lawyer Harmon aboard, in his best courtroom suit of clothes, tall beaver hat and gold-headed cane. The four horses' feet drummed their rat-tat-tat on the hard dirt road, the driver's whip cracked cheerfully. And a front wheel came off!

There was a terrific crash. Never, before or since, has our quiet street heard such a slam-bang, ear-splitting disaster-clatter. Everybody ran, startled, to his front door to see what could have happened.

After this thunderous boom there was an instant of stunned silence, while the shaken-up passengers got their breath. The appalled spectators stared, frozen, wondering if anybody in the wreck could have survived the shock.

And then, like a trumpet, above the cloud of dust hanging over the prostrate stagecoach, rose Lawyer Harmon's voice, his ringing, Daniel Webster courtroom voice. In a resonant bellow, people telling the story often say relishingly, "You c'd ha' heard him in Shaftsbury!"

"WHERE'S MY HAT?" he yelled indignantly.

For us, that shout of his has been a needle-sharp comment on human nature. I felt its prick a year or so ago, when news came over the radio of a tragic loss of life in Japan from a tornado. A great-niece of mine then lived in that country. I asked anxiously, "Anywhere near where Nancy lives?" Someone said, "No, two hundred miles or so away." On which I leaned back, relaxed, with a murmur of relief.

An old member of the family circle knocked the ashes out of his pipe and inquired mildly, "Where's *your* hat?"

Poor Lawyer Harmon! I suppose he had a normal number of good points. But for us, all that is left of his memory stands as a warning signpost.

Altars on the High Places

Back of the Brick Farm House about two miles north of Arlington village is a steep, open hill pasture. Near the top is an extra-fine elm. It is very tall, very old, exceptionally graceful—yet apparently, a century or so ago, it had a hard struggle at the beginning of its life. The seed from which it grew fell on the top of a large flat rock. As it sprouted it must have had mightly little to live on. But the power of growing tree-roots is as prodigious as their growth is slow. Evidently there was a crack in the rock, and the tree-roots, fighting for their lives, slowly split asunder the massive ledge, pushing the two pieces to one side and the other. Now it stands towering above a rock table on each side of its great bole.

Of course a great rock with a flat top suggests "playing house" to any little girl. As a child I often spent the day with my great-uncle's family who lived at the Brick Farm House. At that time—maybe seventy years ago—Charles Crofut's mother, Merwin Crofut's grandmother, Donald Crofut's great-grandmother, was still living. She was born a Hawley and for part of her childhood had been brought up at the Brick Farm House. (The Hawleys and the Canfields have a family connection.) And she looked the part—sweet-faced, white-haired, delicate and refined, very gentle in speech. In those days, children were usually taken once in a while to call on old folks who were family connections. Mostly on such formal visits, children sat silent, dreamily half-listening to the talk of their elders. But one day, I chanced for a moment to be left alone with old Mrs. Crofut. To my surprise the sweet-faced old lady began to talk to me directly. "Do you ever play up in the hill pasture back of the Brick Farm House?"

"Oh yes, very often," I said.

She asked again, "Is the old elm still there, the one with a big flat stone on each side?"

I was astonished that any grown-up knew it. "Oh yes indeed, I often play house there."

She said, musingly, "I used to play up there, too, eighty years ago or so, when I was a little girl, about your age. I always thought those two stones looked like what I imagined altars would look like—in old Bible times."

I nodded my head. I had thought that, too.

She went on, "Well, I had always been bothered because in what the clergyman read from the Bible every Sunday, something was said every once in a while about how wicked it was to have altars and make burnt offerings, on high places. It was all right and pleased God very much when the altars were in the valley—or somewhere on a low place. But the idea of an altar in a *high* place seemed to make Him very cross. You know—you've probably heard it, too, read out in Morning Service. 'Then they offered their sacrifices on every high hill and under green trees, wherefore I, the Lord God, say unto you I shall blow against you the fire of my wrath. Terror shall I turn upon you. Out of heaven shall I thunder upon you. Lightning shall I'—I haven't got the exact words but that was the idea."

Yes, I, too, remembered those angry words raging against praying before altars on the high places, or even going there. I was a couple of generations after old Mrs. Crofut and hadn't been brought up, as she had, to think that in every single sentence in the Bible there is some moral command. But, listening vaguely to the reading of the First Lesson in church, I, too, had wondered what ever could be the matter with high places. But I hadn't wondered enough to bother me.

Just thinking about it still seemed to bother old Mrs. Crofut. She sat up straight in her rocking chair, holding her white head high. "It didn't *scare me*," she said. "It made me mad. I *loved* going up on the high places. And I couldn't see why it was all right to have your altar, and make your sacrifices to God down in the valley, but not up on a high place. I thought to myself, I don't believe a word of it. And then one day I asked my mother why was it wicked to do on a high place and under a green tree something it was all right to do down in the valley. She was churning that day and said, in a surprised voice, 'What? What did you say?' I asked her again why God thought it was wrong to put your altar in a high place.

"My mother looked at the clock and said, trying to be patient, 'Oh, wicked people were the ones who did that, do-go-along-and-play, child.'

"I said, and I suppose I sounded just stubborn, 'I can't see that being in one place and not another makes what you do wrong.'

"My mother said, not at all patiently this time, 'I suppose you think *you* know better than the Bible, about what's wrong and what's right!'

"So I thought I'd try it out, myself. I didn't say any more to my mother. I went out into the pantry and made myself a sandwich out of yesterday's pot roast. Then I climbed up the hill pasture to that elm tree."

The frail old lady bent her transparent face towards the listening child. "I had taken some matches along in the pocket of my apron, and I made a little fire of dry twigs on one of the stones, and I burned the sandwich, bit by bit, in the flames. It took quite a while. But I burned it all."

She leaned back. "As my sacrifice was burning, I kept thinking about the Lord God pouring out His wrath—maybe thunder and lightning from Red Mountain. I tell you, I was scared. But scared or not, I wanted to see for myself." She was silent, looking back into the past.

Fixed in suspense I murmured a question. "What happened?" I asked.

"Not a thing. The cows went on cropping the grass, the calves had a good time kicking up their heels and playing together. The sun shone. The little breeze blew the leaves of the elm tree. Not a bit of notice had been taken from anywhere. I sat on the other stone looking up and down the valley. All my life long it has made me feel good to remember how quiet and peaceful and *nice* it looked! Nobody mad—at anything. And I said to myself, 'I'll never believe another thing— not *really* believe—what anybody anywhere says about what's wicked to do and what's right to do, unless it makes sense to me.'"

After a long time of thinking about this—she had given

me a great deal to think about—I asked her, "Did you ever tell anybody about it?"

She began to sway to and fro peacefully in her rocker, "No, never till now."

After a pause I asked her, "Do you want me not to tell, either?"

She stopped her rocking to think, and then answered me in a very old folk-phrase, "I'd just as leave not as do."

But she has been dead for a long, long time now and I'm seventy-six years old. I don't see that it could—now—do any harm to pass her story along to those whom it obviously concerns—mothers, fathers, teachers—perhaps especially the clergy.

Ham and Eggs!

In old times, hay was mowed by hand, with scythes. Since grass must be cut when it is ready to cut, not left to dry on the stalk, the larger fields were mowed by a crew of neighbors, taking turns to help each other out with one of the biggest chores of the farm-year. They stood in a long line at the side of the field, just far enough from each other so that the long-armed swing of their scythes did not reach the legs of the men on their left, and went across the field like soldiers advancing in steady battle-line. It was hard work in the hot sun, but it was cheerful work, for it had some of the stirringly sociable aspects of other communal get-togethers, like barn-raisings or husking-bees. There was often a man with a gift for inventing jingles, and he made up work-chanties with a strong rhythmic accent to which every man's forward step could be timed.

At least such chanties were cheerful when they were

gathered on the farm of a generous good provider. This was an important item, for the tradition was that mowers had their breakfasts and lunches provided at the home of the farmer whose hay they were cutting. Most farm-families felt put on their mettle and provided the best they had—the traditional heaped-up meat, potatoes and pie. Vermont farmers were bought up to be thrifty, but no farm-family anywhere is likely to eat meagerly.

Yet there was one woman, as the story goes, who was very stingy with her food. On that farm the neighborhood gang assembled soberly. One year, as they came together very early in the morning, to start their mowing while the dew was on the grass, they found that the only food on the long table was a bowl for each man of curds and whey. Since you probably don't know what this dish was, I'll explain that it was what we now call cottage-cheese or pot-cheese, made of sour milk curdled by rennet. It was served in a bowl with the whey which the rennet had separated from the curds. Young children often had it before they were sent to bed.

The men ate this poor, mean fare in silence. Hanging their heads, they went out to the big hayfield and began their work. Soon a dismal chant rose to the ears of those in the farmhouse. Their scythes moved in slow, languid strokes to go with the funereal rhythm, which they sang over and over, as they dragged along:

> "Cu—u—rds and *wh-e-e-y*
> And wo-ork all *day!*"

The woman of the house could not but hear this pointed allusion, could not but see how slowly the scythes were moving. So she sent an extra, mid-morning snack down to the hayfield—a pot of cold baked beans. The disgruntled men gathered hungrily around it. Such a small pot! It didn't take them long to eat what was in it. Putting their heads together to invent a way to show without words how they felt, they ate every bean and polished the bean-pot till the brown pottery of the inside shone, clean and bare. One of the men took it back to the house and waited to see what the farmer's wife would say. She looked down into it, saw its desolate emptiness. But turning the cover over, she saw that a bean had stuck to it. At which she said with satisfaction, "There! Just enough, I see—and one bean over!" In our town that is a proverbial expression.

By that time her husband was ashamed, and insisted that a hearty hot dinner should be ready at noon. Going to the smokehouse, he brought out a big ham. In the pantry stood a row of baked pies meant to carry the family through the whole next week. Every farmhouse always had plenty of eggs; potatoes cost nothing; sliced ham does not take long to fry. The plates of the mowers were heaped high. That was a meal to remember!

After it, the men were so full that they took a brief siesta in the shade during which they devised another plan to show how they now felt. When they went back to their mowing, their heads were held high. The battle-line of their scythes marched across the field so fast that the sun shining on the steel blades flashed like streaks of lightning.

Now their mowing song was no dismal chant. It was in brisk, quick-step, jig-time:

> "*Ham* and eggs! take-*care*-of-your-legs!
> *Ham* and eggs! take-*care*-of-your-legs!"

One Side of My
Great-grandmother's
Character

Almera Hawley Canfield, wife and then widow of Nathaniel Canfield, was my great-grandmother. She died years before I was born but I have heard so much about her from her children and grandchildren and her neighbors that I feel as though I had known her personally.

She was a small, spunky, fiery-hearted woman, with impassioned convictions. One of these was that slavery was wrong. Since she was born in 1785, she was—one might say—decidedly in advance of her times. Yet not in Vermont, where the firmly held conviction that slavery was wrong has existed from the founding of the State. I suppose there is not a child in our Green Mountain schools who does not know that ours was the first written Constitution in the world which made any form of human slavery illegal.

As the feeling about slavery became everywhere hotter and

hotter, pro and con, my great-grandmother's feelings grew hotter. I always understood from her sons, my great-uncles, that she had made some financial contribution to John Brown's expedition to Harper's Ferry. As she never had much money, this meant a good deal. But I'm not sure that anybody had any proof of this. At any rate, my father several times told me the story of his being waked up very early one morning when he was a lad in his middle 'teens, to see his grandmother, fully dressed, leaning over his bed and shaking his shoulder to wake him. She said, "Get up, Jim, this is the day John Brown is to be hanged. And I want you to go over and toll the bell for him."

My father said he was so much startled by her gray face and trembling hands that he turned out of bed in a jiffy and got into his clothes. She sent him across the street (for the brick house which is now the Community House was my great-grandmother's home) and up into the belfry of St. James. There, obeying her because he didn't dare not to, he began to toll the bell very slowly, as it was always tolled to announce a death. He hadn't had any breakfast, and he got very tired of doing it, but he didn't dream of stopping. About two hours later, another Arlington boy appeared climbing up the steps to the belfry roof. He, too, looked startled and round-eyed, and said as he took the bell rope from my father's hands, "It's my turn. Aunt Almera said toll." He began pulling the bell—one great strong stroke, and then a pause while you counted to get the strokes even. That was the way a funeral was always announced. My father went downstairs and across the street and had his breakfast. Nobody said a word to him about the bell ringing. His grandmother sat in the front parlor, listening to make sure the tolling was continuously done, and reading the Bible—the Old Testament part.

In that way the bell was kept tolling all day long, one big boy after another being sent up by Great-grandmother. By the middle of the morning the people from out in the country districts, wondering what in the world could have happened, had one after another hitched up their horses and come in to town to inquire from anybody out on the sidewalk who was dead. They were told to go into the brick house and ask old Mrs. Canfield. When they did, they found Great-grandmother sitting in her little straight rocker, the big Bible on her knees, reading aloud the most awful texts from the Old Testament, the ones which called down vengeance on evil-doers. She stopped long enough to tell them what the tolling meant, then went on reading aloud those savage expressions of hatred of evildoers.

When night came she allowed the tolling to stop.

But my father always said that for years afterward on still days, or when he first woke up at dawn, he could hear that heart-shaking, Day-of-Wrath knell, solemnly filling with its deep resonance all our corner of the Vermont valley.

One of my great-grandmother's sons was my grandfather, who was for many years an Episcopal clergyman, pastor of a New York parish. Of course there were a good many people in his sophisticated city parish who were not as hot about abolition as his mother. My grandfather was a scholarly man, who knew a great deal about history and a great deal about politics, and who had a judicious turn of mind, which made it possible for him to see two sides of the question, even a very vital one.

Because he was a practiced speaker, he was not infrequently asked to speak in Arlington on some special occasion like the Fourth of July celebration. One time after the close of the

Civil War he was thus the orator of the day. The upper part of the Town Hall, which was then the gathering place for assemblies in Arlington, was filled with people who had come to celebrate the day and to hear Dr. Eli. His old mother, my great-grandmother, sat in the front row, very proud of her tall, knowledgeable son, speaking from the platform.

But in the course of his address he chanced to say, in speaking of the causes of the Civil War, something about "that fanatic, John Brown," a phrase which was common then among people who deplored the horrible, bloody tragedy of the Civil War, even though it proved in the end to have been necessary.

But this was more than his mother could stand. Springing to her feet, she called out in a loud voice, *"Shame! Shame!"* And gathering her shawl around her shoulders, she marched down the middle aisle to the door and slammed it behind her.

Now in connection with this episode there is an interesting little commentary on human memory and local tradition. My brother and I both remember hearing the story ever so many times when we were young. He remembers it quite distinctly as having taken place inside St. James Church. And I remember with equal distinctness that it was told as taking place in the Town Hall. I consider that I have some real proof on my side, in that the door at the end of the aisle in St. James through which she had to pass to go out is a swinging door and she couldn't slam it! Whereas the Town Hall door always slammed with a resounding, satisfying clangor.

But perhaps the important thing is that both my brother and I remember the rest of the story just as I have set it down here.

Two Wymans

Many of the remembered and quoted Arlington stories are, by implication, sharp comments on human behavior. But many are not. Some of them are remembered just because they are grotesque. Some because they have the great virtue of being unexpected.

One which is told is about a couple of elderly farmers—they were Wymans both of them—who chanced to meet at the top of a steep, stony hill pasture, one of those where cobblestones lie so thickly that, as an old saying put it, "the sheep have to have their noses sharpened to get at the grass between the stones." It was in 1861. Reports of the disastrous first battle of Bull Run had just come in. Northern readers of the newspapers were horrified by the Federal Army's retreat on the run, before the Confederates. In Vermont people spoke of little else. These Wymans sat down to talk over the news.

"Looks bad, don't it?"

"What *do* y' suppose will happen next?"

"S'pose those Southerners come right on up north?"

"What's to hinder?"

There was a silence. Then one old man said, looking down the white road winding off along the valley towards the outside world, "What could *we* do? S'pose right now, we sh'd look down that road, and see thousands of Southern soldiers on it with guns over their shoulders and bayonets and cannon and everything—a hull army of 'em, a-marching up towards Rutland. What could we *do?* No artillery—no ammunition, no guns except for shootin' squirrel! Most all the able-bodied men gone."

The two stooped, gray-haired men gazed down at the imaginary enemies approaching from the south.

But one of them straightened his shoulders valiantly. His eye had been caught by the cobblestones covering the hill below them. Turning to his cousin, he exclaimed, "By gol! We c'd *stun* 'em!"

This incident, which catches the eye no more than a bit of gray lichen on a rock, has never before been written down. I have heard it many times, but always in some neighbor's laughing voice. But even as that laugh sounds in the ear of memory, I now hear in it an overtone of dogged, stubborn courage. Perhaps even this tiny scrap from the past has been, all these years, one of those comments on human behavior which make up tradition.

The Washed Window

Older people in Arlington have a special interest in the last house you pass as you leave our village to drive to Cambridge. It was built and lived in for many years by our first local skilled cabinetmaker. In the early days nearly every house had one good piece of professionally made furniture, brought up from Connecticut on horseback or in an oxcart. These were highly treasured. But the furniture made here was, for the first generation after 1764, put together by men who just wanted chairs, beds, and a table for the family meals—and those as fast as they could be slammed into shape.

For many years Silas Knapp lived in that last house practicing his remarkable skill. Nearly every house of our town acquired in those years one or two pieces of his workmanship. They are now highly prized as "early nineteenth-century, locally made antiques."

He not only made many a fine chest of drawers and bedside

stand there: he also brought up a fine family of children. You may never have noticed this house as you drove by, but once, some twenty or thirty years ago, a great American leader, who chanced to pass through Vermont, asked to be shown the old Knapp home. He had been delivering an important address to a large audience in Rutland. When he stood in front of the small low old house he took off his hat and bowed his gray head in silence. Then he explained to the person who had driven him down to Arlington, "For me it is a shrine."

This is the story back of his visit to the plain little early nineteenth-century artisan's house which to him was a shrine. Viola Knapp was one of the Vermont girls who "went South to teach," taking along with her the attitude towards life she had been brought up to respect. She married there—as the saying goes, "married well"—an army officer of good family. It was a happy, lifelong mating. Viola Knapp Ruffner and her husband, General Ruffner, lived here and there in various cities and towns and brought up a family of five children. It was while the Ruffners were living in West Virginia that—but I'll set the story down as I heard it in my youth, about sixty years ago, from the lips of the distinguished American educator who, as a boy, had been a student of Viola Knapp Ruffner. In his later years, he became one of my father's valued friends.

This is about as he used to tell it to us with many more details than I ever saw told in print. "I never knew exactly how old I was when I first saw Mrs. Ruffner, for in the days of slavery, family records—that is, black-family records—were seldom kept. But from what I have been able to learn, I was born, a slave, on a Virginia plantation, about 1858. In my youth, my home was a log cabin about fourteen by sixteen feet square. We slept on frowsy piles of filthy rags, laid on the dirt floor. Until I was quite a big youth I wore only one garment, a shirt made out of agonizingly rough refuse-flax. We slaves ate corn bread and pork, because those foods could be grown on the plantation without cash expense. I had never seen anything except the slave quarters on the plantation where I was born, with a few glimpses of the 'big house' where our white owners lived. I cannot remember ever, during my childhood and youth, not one single time, when our family sat down together at a table to eat a meal as human families do. We ate as animals do, whenever and wherever an edible morsel was found. We usually took our food up in our fingers, sometimes from the skillet, sometimes from a tin plate held on our knees, and as we chewed on it, we held it as best we could in our hands.

"Life outside our cabin was as slovenly and disordered as inside. The white owners made no effort to keep things up. They really could not. Slaves worked; hence any form of work was too low for white people to do. Since white folks did no work, they did not know how work should be done. The untaught slaves, wholly ignorant of better standards, seldom got around to mending the fences, or putting back a lost hinge on a sagging gate or door. Weeds grew wild everywhere, even in the yard. Inside the big house, when a piece of plastering fell from a wall or ceiling, it was a long time before anybody could stir himself to get it replastered.

"After the end of the Civil War, when we were no longer slaves, my family moved to a settlement near a salt mine, where, although I was still only a child, I was employed— often beginning my day's work at four in the morning. There, we lived in even more dreadful squalor, for our poor rickety cabin was in a crowded slum, foul with unspeakable dirt— literal and moral. As soon as I grew a little older and stronger,

I was shifted from working in the salt mine to a coal mine.
Both mines were then owned by General Lewis Ruffner.

"By that time I had learned my letters and could, after a
fashion, read. Mostly I taught myself, but with some irregular
hours spent in a Negro night school, after an exhausting day's
work in the mines. There were no public schools for ex-slaves;
the poor, totally unequipped, bare room where colored people,
young and old, crowded in to learn their letters was paid for
by tiny contributions from the Negroes themselves.

"About that time I heard two pieces of news, which were like
very distant, very faint glimmers in the blackness of the coal
mine in which nearly all my waking hours were spent. One
was about a school for colored students—Hampton Institute
it was—where they could learn more than their letters. The
other was that the wife of General Ruffner was from Vermont
and that she took an interest in the education of the colored
people who worked for her. I also heard that she was so 'strict'
that nobody could suit her, and that the colored boys who
entered her service were so afraid of her, and found her so
impossible to please, that they never stayed long. But the pay
was five dollars a month, and keep. That was better than the
coal mine—and there was also the chance that she might be
willing to have me go on learning. I got up my courage to
try. What could be worse than the way I was living and the
hopelessness of anything better in the future?

"But I can just tell you that, great, lumbering, muscle-bound
coal-mining boy that I was, I was trembling when I went to
ask for that work. The Ruffners had just moved into an old
house that had been empty for some time, and they were not
yet established, their furniture not unpacked, the outbuildings
not repaired. When I first saw her, Mrs. Ruffner was writing
on an improvised desk which was a plank laid across two kegs.

"I falteringly told her I had come to ask for work. She turned in her chair and looked at me silently. Nobody had ever looked at me like that, not at my rags and dirt but as if she wanted to see what kind of person I was. She had clear, steady gray eyes, I remember. Then she said, 'You can try.' After reflection, she went on, 'You might as well start in by cleaning the woodshed. It looks as though it hadn't been touched for years.'

"She laid down her pen and took me through a narrow side-passage into the woodshed. It was dark and cluttered with all kinds of dirty, dusty things. A sour, moldy smell came up from them. Great cobwebs hung down from the rough rafters of the low, sloping roof. Stepping back for a moment, she brought out a dustpan and a broom. A shovel leaned against the woodshed wall. She put that in my hand and said, 'Now go ahead. Put the trash you clean out on that pile in the yard and we'll burn it up later. Anything that won't burn, like broken glass, put into that barrel.' Then she turned away and left me.

"You must remember that I never had done any work except rough, unskilled heavy labor. I had never cleaned a room in my life, I had never seen a clean room in my life. But I was used to doing as I was told, and I was dead set on managing to go ahead with learning more than I would in that poor beginners' schoolroom. So I began taking out things which anybody could see were trash, like mildewed rags, which fell apart into damp shreds the minute I touched them. There were also, I remember, some moldy heaps of I don't know what, garbage maybe, that had dried into shapeless chunks of bad-smelling filth. In one corner was the carcass of a long-dead dog, which I carried out to the pile of trash in the side yard. Glass was everywhere, broken and unbroken empty whiskey bottles, bits of crockery ware. These I swept with the broom and picking up my sweepings in my hands (I had no idea what the dust-pan was for) carried them outside.

"The shed looked to me so much better that I went in to find Mrs. Ruffner. She was still writing. I told her, 'I cleaned it.' Pushing back her chair she went out to the woodshed with me.

"She made no comment when she first opened the door and looked around her with clear gray eyes. Then she re-marked quietly, 'There's still some things to attend to. Those pieces of wood over there, you might pile up against the wall in the corner. They would do to burn. Be sure to clean the floor well before you start piling the wood on it. And here's another pile of rotten rags, you see. And that tangle behind the door. You'd better pull it all apart and see what's there. Throw away the trash that's mixed with it.' She turned to go back, saying, 'Just keep on till you've got it finished and then come and tell me.'

"She didn't speak kindly. She didn't speak unkindly. I looked at the woodshed with new eyes and saw that, sure enough, I'd only made a beginning. I began to pull at the odds and ends in that dusty mess behind the door. And to my astonishment I felt I was perspiring. The work wasn't hard for me, you understand it. It was like little boy's play com-pared to the back-breaking labor I had always done. And it wasn't that I minded carrying around in my bare hands things slimy with rot or having liquid filth drip on my ragged pants. I was used to dirt, and my hands were as calloused as my feet. What made me sweat was the work I had to do with my mind. Always before, when somebody had given me a piece of work to do, he had stood right there to do all the thinking. Here his orders would have been, 'Pull that piece of sacking out. That stick, put it on top of the woodpile. Those dried-up chicken bones, scrape them up from the dirt and throw them in the trash pile.' All I would have had to do was to plod along, doing what I was ordered. Now I was the one to give the orders.

"Now that I was really thinking about what I was doing, I was amazed to see how little I had done, how much more there was to do than I had seen.

"I stooped to pull apart the grimy, mud-colored tangle heaped up back of the door. As I stirred it, a snake crawled out from under it and wriggled towards the door. A big fellow. I wasn't surprised. I was used to snakes. I dropped a stone on his head and carried his long, black body out to the trash pile in the yard.

"Now I had come to a corner where chickens evidently roosted every night. Everything was covered with their droppings, like smearing of white paint. I thought nothing of handling them, and taking up the body of one I found lying still and dead in the midst of the rubbish. More rotted rags, a stained, torn pair of pants, too far gone even for me to wear, still smelling foul. Some pieces of wood, not rotten, fit for fuel. Everything I came to had first to be pulled loose from the things it was mixed up with, and enough of the dirt shaken off to let me make out what it was. And then I had to think what to do with it. No wonder that the sweat ran down my face. To see, I had to wipe my eyes with the back of my hands.

"Finally, the last of the refuse was taken apart and cleared away and the litter and filth which had dropped from it to the floor was swept together and carried out to the trash pile. I kept looking over my shoulder for somebody to make the decisions, to tell me what to do. 'Throw that away. Save that. Put it with the firewood. Toss that into the barrel with the broken glass.' But there was nobody there to give me orders. I went in to get Mrs. Ruffner. 'I got it done,' I told her.

"Laying down her pen, she came again to see. I felt nervous as, silent and attentive, she ran those clear eyes of hers over what I had been doing. But I wasn't at all prepared to have her say again, 'That's better, but there's a great deal still to do. You haven't touched the cobwebs, I see.' I looked up at them, my lower jaw dropped in astonishment. Sure enough, there they hung in long, black festoons. I had not once lifted my head to see them. 'And how about washing the window? Here, step in here and get a pail of water for that. Here are some clean rags. You'll have to go over it several times to get it clean.'

"She went back into the house and I stood shaken by more new ideas than I could tell you. I hadn't even noticed there was a window, it was so thick with dust and cobwebs. I had never had anything to do with a glass window. In the dark cabins I had lived in, the windows were just holes cut in the walls.

"I set to work once more, the sweat running down my face. Suppose she wouldn't even let me try to do her work. I never could get into Hampton! What if I just never could get the hang of her ways? Stricken, scared, I began again to clean that woodshed! I went over and over every corner of it. Once in a while I stopped stock-still to *look* at it, as I had never looked at anything before, trying really to see it. I don't know that ever in my life afterwards did I care about doing anything right as much as getting that little old woodshed clean.

"When I came to what I thought was the end, I stopped to get my breath. I looked up at the slanting roof. The rafters were not only cleared of cobwebs but bare of dust; the floor was swept clean, not a chip, not a thread, not a glint of broken glass on it. Piles of firewood against the walls. And the window! *I* had washed that window! Five times I had washed it. How it sparkled! How the strong sunshine poured through it! Now the woodshed was no rubbish pile. It was a room. To me it looked like a parlor. I was proud of it. Till then I had never been proud of anything I had done.

"Then for the third time I went to call Mrs. Ruffner to inspect. Big boy as I was, twice her size, my hands were shaking, my lips twitching. I felt sick. Had I done it right this time? Could I ever do anything right?

"I watched her face as she passed my work in review, looking carefully up, down, and around. Then she turned to me and, looking straight into my eyes, she nodded and said, 'Now it's clean. Nobody could have done it any better.'

"She had opened the door through which I took my first step towards civilized standards of living."

He drew a long breath and went on, "For a year and a half I lived with those standards around me, working for Mrs. Ruffner. What I learned from her! It was like breathing new air. I could never say in words what she taught me, for it was not taught in words but in life. She never pronounced such abstract expressions as 'frankness' and 'honesty'—they radiated from her, like sunlight streaming silently through a clean window, as she spoke of the tasks she set me. They were so simple she took them for granted, but they were revelations to me. I have repeated ever so many times the story of what Mrs. Ruffner taught me by the way she lived in her home—lessons of as great a value to me as any education I ever had in all my life. To anybody seeing me from the outside, I would, I suppose, have seemed to be learning only how to clean a filthy yard, how to keep a fence in repair, how to hang a gate straight, how to paint a weather-beaten barn.

"And then how to study—how to learn from the books she helped me secure, the books she took for granted and which, for me, were revelations. She took my breath away by suggesting, casually, that I begin to have a library of my own. Me!

"It was an old dry-goods box. I knocked the boards out of one side, used them for shelves, and with Mrs. Ruffner's backing to steady me, began with incredulous pride to set up, side by side, one and another of the battered, priceless printed volumes which, under Mrs. Ruffner's roof, I had come to own. I owning books!

"And yet, after all, later on when the way ahead was darkly blocked, it was that woodshed which pushed open the door.

"It would take too long to tell you all the piled-up difficulties I had to climb over to reach my goal of a real school with real, full-time classroom study. All sorts of things happened as I made my way over the long distance which separated me from Hampton. And when I actually stood before that three-story, brick school building, it looked as though I would not be allowed to enter it as a student. My trip had been longer, harder, had cost more than I had dreamed it could. I was nearly penniless, footsore, dusty, gaunt, unwashed.

"The teacher who was in charge of admitting or turning away students gave me a long, doubtful look and told me to wait. Well, I waited. I saw her interviewing other students, better dressed, cleaner, ever so much more promising-looking than I, without a look at me. But I didn't go away. That solid, three-story brick building—all just to provide a chance to study for people who had never had a chance to study—how could I go away, even if I were not welcome? I waited. After several hours of watching that teacher admitting other students, she finally had an idea about me and told me briefly, dubiously, 'The classroom next to this one needs to be cleaned before the Institute opens tomorrow. Do you suppose you could sweep it out? There's a broom over there in the corner.'

"In all my life I never had an order which so uplifted my heart. Could I sweep it out? Oh, Mrs. Ruffner!

"I swept that classroom three times. I moved every piece of furniture and swept under each one. There was a closet. I swept that. Joyfully I swept every corner clean. I found a dust cloth. I dusted everything in the room, I turned the cloth and dusted everything again, and again. I was in the middle of my fourth dusting when the teacher opened the door and stepped in. She was a Yankee. She knew what to look for. She took a clean handkerchief from her pocket, shook it out, and passed it over the top of a desk. After one startled look at me, she rubbed the seat of a chair with it.

"I stood at ease, my head high, fearing nothing. I did not need anybody's permission to feel sure of myself. I had been asked to perform a task. I had done it.

"She passed her testing handkerchief over a window sill, and turned to face me. She was a Yankee and wasted no words. She put the handkerchief back in her pocket, and in a matter-of-fact voice said, 'You're admitted to Hampton.'

"I had been set an entrance examination. And thanks to Mrs. Ruffner I had passed it."

His name was Booker T. Washington.

Two Lovely, Silly Girls
of Long Ago

Vermonters always read with a smile—sometimes lay the book down to laugh outright—the occasional phrase casually used by a historian, when he speaks of the "sour, grimly Puritan streak" in the early days of our Green Mountain communities. We, the great-grandchildren of those life-loving, rough-and-ready, dancing and joking and danger-enjoying young rebels from the sober life they had left behind them in the older settlements of New England, we know that mighty little straight-laced, Puritan gloom darkened their forward-looking lives. There was plenty of game here, the streams were full of trout, the lakes of larger fish, it was as close to a sports paradise as any hunter's wish-thoughts could desire, and hardly a Vermonter who did not revel in hunting and fishing, and the consequent good eating. All feet were nimble for the noisy rhythmic cheerfulness of dancing. Older people, now living, sometimes say, describing an old neighborhood on a back road now quiet and abandoned, "My grandmother always told me that you could, any evening you felt like it, summer or winter, step out of your back door, give a good blast on a conch-shell and call in twenty couples and a fiddler from neighbors near enough to hear you, to stamp it out in your big kitchen till midnight, in reels and square dances. Everybody in those days was ready for fun—a barn-raising bee or a husking or a sugaring-off was the best kind of a party."

That sounds as though "the fun" of those days was always rustic, with a bark on, slap-stick, of the haw-haw kind, described by social historians as "folk-ways." We don't know exactly what they mean by that, but to our ears, it has a disdainful association of near-illiteracy, primitive narrowness of outlook, and ignorance of ordinary good manners in social relations. But from the early founding of town libraries all over the Green Mountains, and the lively diversity of the books in them (in the first Arlington Library of 1806, Gibbon's *Decline and Fall of the Roman Empire* was among the first books purchased, along with the then-popular sensational thriller, *The Mysteries of Udolpho*), we know our ancestors were book-users beyond the general average, as Vermonters still are; and that they thought and talked of much more than farm and village gossip.

As for the perfect naturalness in them of a social life which, in its usages and manners and vocabulary, was probably then called "polite" and now "conventional," we have proofs in the many letters, diaries and memoirs from those days still preserved in back bureau drawers, or occasionally turned up in our attics. I quote from a letter from a Virginian written in 1777:

SIR,

Before I left Virginia, I had conceived a very indifferent opinion of the Northern states, and especially of the state of Vermont. I had formed the idea of rough barren country, inhabited by a fierce, uncivilized and very unpolished people. I made my tour ... I was surprised and astonished beyond measure to find a fertile, luxuriant soil, cultivated by a virtuous, industrious, and civilized set of inhabitants; many of whom lived in taste and elegance, and appeared not unacquainted with the polite arts.... The rapid progress in population and improvement, and the many surprising incidents that have taken place during the short period of your existence as a state, will furnish material for some able historian, to give the world an history that shall be both entertaining and instructive.

And in contrast to these measured formal eighteenth-century cadences, here are some extracts from letters accidentally found in an old house, where recently, in remodeling the attic, part of the floor was taken up. There, very dusty, lay some pages from the correspondence of two deliciously silly, lively, beau-catching girls at the "young lady" age, about one hundred and forty years ago. They were written for each other's eyes only, and hence are of the most unstudied artlessness. The vocabulary has more dictionary words in it, and less slang, than girls of today would use in writing about their boy friends; but the spirit is quite strikingly the same.

ARLINGTON, VERMONT
MAY 24, 1818

MY DEAR COUSIN:

When I wrote you last, I fondly flattered myself that I should be with you by this time [one of these girls still lived in the old home in Connecticut] but I see no possibility of my going at present or in the way we talked of. [There was of course no regular passenger service between Arlington and western Connecticut at that time.] I regret very much that your home town cannot furnish you with the command of *one beau* that you could send for me but perhaps you have not ambition enough to exercise all the *power* you might have over them.

You conclude that I am engaged in matrimony—how preposterous! I am pretty well convinced that I do not possess "captivating charms" sufficient to make any serious impression on the hearts of the Arlington beaux. Your apprehensions about my heart are groundless. I believe it to be as tender as ever it was.

Mrs. Deming's cousin has for some time been absent from here, returned last week. I have seen him only once since he returned. Mrs. Deming says she *thinks* matrimony is very foreign from his mind at present. I have not had an opportunity of conversing with him alone on the subject. He confines himself very much to his *business* and *books*.

Sister Laura has an addition of another son to her family and I have for the week past been officiating as nurse. I have to steal time to write this. I trust, my dear friend, you will throw "the mantle of charity" over its numerous imperfections. Laura sends love to you and says I must tell you she is very sensible of the pleasantness of her situation here in Arlington. It is agreeable to have a church near; and to have a store directly opposite, furnished not only with the *necessaries,* but the *elegancies and ornaments of life* is delightful indeed. [We Arlington people knowing the merchandise offered by our "general store" have always smiled over this description which seemed absurdly florid; but recently one of us, projecting himself into the past more accurately, has suggested that it may not be so comic as it sounds. Perhaps in 1818, thirty years before the railroad was brought in, with its total rearrangement of community life, Arlington, at the crossroads as it was of the "through" stagecoach line from Boston to Albany and from New York to Montreal, may well have had more amply furnished shops than the old Connecticut rural towns in the isolated western part of that state.]

The hills of Arlington are just beginning to put on their green attire. How I wish you was here [the only grammatical mistake in the letters] to wander about with me and some clever beaux to admire their beauty.

Clarissa, if you can forgive this scroll of nonsense, I can assure you I will write again as soon as possible.

Yours forever,
CLARISSA NORTON

From another letter:

ARLINGTON, JULY 12, 1818
MY DEAR CLARISSA,

We have so much company here, and my time and attention is so taken up, that I have very little time to devote to writing or even thinking of absent friends. Immediately after I wrote you last I heard that Mr. B. did not intend going to Connecticut at all for some reasons, and consequently I had given up all hope of again seeing you in Goshen. My anticipated happiness was destroyed and I was foolish enough to cry with vexation. The prospect at present wears a more favorable aspect. Laura has just returned from a visit of several days to Bennington. She brings word that Mr. B. intends going in the fall and I may depend on going with him but I dare not calculate much upon it for fear of being disappointed. How I wish you would put Ann's plan in execution. Conquer your scruples regarding the loss of your heart. You would not value the loss of your heart very much if you could have one of the best of our Green Mountain boys in return. I wish I could insure you one. *Some* say Cousin S.F.'s heart is in Vermont, *others* say in Connecticut. I have endeavored to ascertain the truth of it but have not been able.

With respect to my own, I believe it to be perfectly safe and sound. I presume there is none that would wish to deprive me of it.

Cousin, can you think it possible that Sister E. has dismissed her faithful lover? Sally Dewey was lately married to ——— Brush who is that darling boy that you publicly ———. Don't be married before I see you.

Unalterably yours,

C. NORTON

[These letters are from the great-grandmother of Richard K. Miles, now head of a business in Arlington. The Miles family have since the eighteenth century come and gone from western Connecticut to Arlington, Vermont. One aspect to note in these girl-boy letters is the complete absence in them of any of the conventional, set formulae of piety, which have a large part in any "Puritan" letters of this period which have come down from many of the old New England settlements.]

LATER NINETEENTH
CENTURY AND
TWENTIETH CENTURY

A "Character"

Like all groups of human beings, everywhere, Arlington has had its share of oddities. In meaningful folk-talk, they are called "characters."

One of these characters was Mrs. Burdette. She lived in the long, low, very old house, now the Rectory of St. James. Her husband had been a blacksmith. (At that time, the family name had been Burdit.) Her only son got a job working for the New York Central Railway when that company was a fairly new organization. He was a capable and industrious man, and rose gradually, first to be paymaster and, in the end, one of their vice-presidents. Such transformation as that from a blacksmith's son to be high official in a large corporation was part of the American way of life in the nineteenth century as now. The family name became, at this time, Burdette.

As long as Mrs. Burdette had her husband and son to

take care of, she lived like any other New England house-keeper, and home-maker. But her husband died, and some years after, her son went to live in New York where his work was, leaving her alone in the old Vermont village. Then, to everyone's surprise, Mrs. Burdette looked with a fresh eye and an original mind at her way of life.

What she saw—evidently, from the way of life she then adopted—was that the rules of housekeeping had been set up to meet the differing needs of a family composed of old and young, men and women, living together in one unit under one roof; but that custom had set and hardened those rules in that pattern, as though it were not just a working compromise but a sacred ritual. The ancient Greeks, in their great classical century and later, went on building their stone temples in the pattern which had been the only one available in earlier periods when everything was made of wood; the first designers of automobiles constructed their gasoline-propelled cars with a dashboard because that had been necessary in earlier periods to protect the passengers in the front seat of the vehicle from mud flung back by equine hoofs. I don't at all claim that Mrs. Burdette thought of the matter in these theoretical terms. But she must have perceived, with or without conscious awareness, that home-making for one older woman might well be carried on in a pattern different from that formalized by the needs of families of six to twelve persons. She threw away the traditional notes by which good housekeeping had always been played, and did hers by ear.

Why ever in the world, for instance, three meals a day? To everyone who spoke disapprovingly (and there were many such, of course) about the fantastic irregularity of her meal-times, she said she was sick and tired of sitting down to eat at hours when, maybe, she wasn't a bit hungry, and then feeling empty as a drum at times when no food was available. Since she had only herself to look out for, she began to prepare her meals when she felt like eating. Sometimes when she woke up early, she had breakfast at half-past three in the morning. If she chanced to sleep late, at ten or eleven. She ate according to her appetite. "Why not?" she asked people. She certainly throve on this relaxed, flexible schedule. Never did a woman of her age look less tired and harassed.

She treated the necessity for sleep in very much the same original fashion. On this subject her declaration of independence ran about as follows: "All my life, I've lain awake for hours in my bed, when there were ever so many things I'd like to do, around the house. Then the next day I've been half dead with sleepiness when I had to keep going. Now I'm going to sleep when I feel like sleeping. And I'm going to get up when I don't feel sleepy any longer."

To facilitate this, and to get rid of the bother of always undressing and dressing, her outer garment was from that time on made of black surah silk. This was a soft fabric which didn't crumple as much as most fabrics of the time. She had grown stout as she grew older, and her black surah dresses were always made with loose, ample folds, a little like an academic gown. If she began to feel sleepy at eight o'clock in the morning, she took a few steps to the nearest sofa in her living room, lay down on it and fell asleep like a child. If she didn't thus drop into exquisite slumber, she got up and went out to weed her flower beds, for she was an excellent gardener.

I well remember the odd feeling children had, who were sent over on errands, to find Mrs. Burdette sleeping soundly in her black silk dress on the sofa in her living room as if in her own bedroom. A piece of paper and a pencil always lay on the table. If we found her sleeping, we wrote down what we were to tell her.

Her idea was that her black surah silk dresses wouldn't crumple. She was mistaken. They did. But since her eyes were dimmed by age, she didn't see this. And no harm done. Living next door to St. James as she did, the loud booming of its bell to call people to Sunday morning service fairly rocked her house. If she was asleep, sometimes she heard it, sometimes she didn't. When she did, she got up, put on her bonnet, tied the strings under her chin, and without once looking in the mirror, went over and took her place in her pew. Maybe you can imagine how she looked! But we were all so used to her that what we mostly saw and what we now remember was her fresh-colored, calm, old face, almost unlined, always ready to smile.

Once one of the traveling salesmen who came and went here stayed overnight in the Arlington Inn. He was troubled about something in his business and a poor sleeper anyhow as he used to say, telling the story, so that he lay tense, fagged, wide-awake in his bed, trying to be still in spite of his restlessness. Finally about half-past two, he gave up, dressed and went out into the mild black summer night to see if exercise would quiet his straining nerves.

The windows of the long, low house just across the street were yellow with lamp-light. Thinking that perhaps someone was sick or needed help, he walked over there. Through an uncurtained window he saw a stout old woman, cleaning her pantry shelves. (Mrs. Burdette's house was always as clean as anybody's.) She had lifted the dishes down to the kitchen table and was now laying clean strips of white paper on the shelves. The taut, weary, morose insomniac watched her for a time, but as she didn't look sick—quite the contrary, rosy and remarkably cheerful—he set out "around the block" (as we always say of our one block) to School Street and back again to the hotel on Main Street.

But the lights were still on in the house across the street. His curiosity was aroused. What could be going on? It was then about three in the morning. He crossed once more to stand in the darkness outside, and look in through the window. The stout old lady in black had now moved into the next room, and still in her gingham apron was sitting in front of a parlor organ, pumping the pedals with her feet, playing and singing. The window was closed and he could not catch what song it was, but apparently the words brought back some lively memories from her long-ago youth, for as she sang, her fresh old face creased into mirth and she stopped to laugh.

My great-uncle Zadok Canfield was born so early in the nineteenth century that he was brought up on the jingling couplets which eighteenth-century folk used to call poetry. One of these he used to quote whenever some troubled, exasperated good housekeeper cried out on the absurd way Nellie Burdette lived.

In a loud, sing-song chant Uncle Zed would intone,

> "Small habits well pursued betimes
> Can reach the magnitude of crimes,"

and never bothered to see whether he was understood or not.

Can't Leave My Horses...!

Sometimes, in telling these tales of our old mountain town, I speak as though, varied as they are, we had all agreed on the meaning of each one, in so far as it is a comment on life. Of course, this is not so. The color of any event is, for its observer, determined far more by the associations connected with it.

Up here, where marble is the commonest rock, the water is apt to be full of lime, and is not loved by good housekeepers. In every kitchen there used to be an old-fashioned pump which brought soft rain water up from the cistern for washing. You couldn't imagine a more prosaic object, could you, than a battered, iron kitchen-pump over a kitchen sink. But I remember an old neighbor telling me that she had the pump taken clean out of her kitchen and went without rain water all her life because, when she was a little girl, it was there that she overheard her father, standing with his hand on the top of the pump, tell her mother that he was going away that day, to enlist in the Union Army to fight in the Civil War. He never came back, shot in the first battle he entered. In the little girl's mind, the sight of the pump was so associated with the horror on her mother's young face as she heard her husband's decision, that, even as an old woman, speaking of that memory, she cried out, "It made me sick to look at the thing."

In the same way, although the comment on human life made by our folk-memories is perfectly plain, and although, in general, most of us take these stories as having the same meaning, there are for some of us associations which radically change the color of an anecdote. Not always tragically.

Once when I was a child, little enough to become absorbed in cutting out paper dolls, I was sitting on a foot stool with my scissors and a page of gaily colored paper dolls in the spare bedroom of a neighbor of ours. This ground-floor room was mostly used as a sort of extra workroom. The sewing machine was placed in it, and a big table for cutting out garments. On that spring morning, my neighbor's young married daughter sat vigorously pushing the treadle. Like haste made audible, the needle flew up and down in some thin, white material which lay in heaps around her and around the machine. My aunt had come to visit with the mother, bringing me along with her. The two older women sat in low chairs in front of the open windows. They were talking about things which interest a little girl much less than paper dolls, so I haven't the faintest memory of what they said. The needle of the machine stabbed up and down as it sped through the thin material. The young wife whose feet nervously pushed the treadle to and fro often glanced up at the clock which hung on the wall. From this, I guessed, without much interest, she had a noon-meal to prepare at home and no time to spare. The murmur of the older women's voices as they bent their heads over their knitting came dimly to the little girl absorbed with scissors and paper.

Into this quiet, feminine room came my neighbor's son-in-law, the husband of the young woman hurrying the sewing machine along.

He said to his wife, "Eppie, I've got to go up to the Mac Pringle pasture this morning to make sure the fences are all right before I turn the young stock out there. The grass must be high enough for them now. Don't you want to come along for the walk? It must be nice up there—a four-county view, I bet, it's so clear."

The young wife stopped the whirring of the sewing machine, and, one hand still holding the material in line with the needle, looked up, her face blank with surprise at the interruption. When she had taken in his idea, she cried out, "Oh, Paul, I couldn't possibly. Not this morning. I've got all these curtains to hem before Aunt Deborah gets here."

Her tall husband, standing broad-shouldered in the doorway, his fair hair nearly touching the top, looked at her and said, not urgently, rather dreamily, almost as if speaking to himself, "It'll be nice up there, Eppie. I bet strawberry blossoms are out everywhere. And the wild cherries are in bloom."

The young wife's face took on a distracted look. She said, looking back at the shining needle, standing stock-still in the stuff, "But I just figured, at the rate I'm going, I can get these curtains hemmed and hung before Aunt Debbie comes for her visit."

For a long moment her husband looked at her in apparent

seriousness. Then he said with an even, unemphatic accent, "Can't leave your horses, can you?"

I was watching this little dialogue, and I still remember the strange mixture of expressions on the wife's young, comely face—exasperation, impatience, a sort of outraged incredulity —but something else, too. She looked hard at her husband, her eyes searching his. He had his straw hat in his hands, and now tossed it to her with a light-hearted gesture of buffoonery, "Here, I'll let you wear my hat so you won't lose any time going to fetch yours."

The young wife sprang up so roughly that her chair fell over backward. She did not pick it up. She left the curtain material to fall, billowing, where it would, on the sewing machine, on the floor. "Oh, *you!*" she said in a tone of extreme irritability. But her expression was not one which went with it.

She caught the hat, and crammed it on her own pretty head. Her husband smiled broadly and turned to go. With a darting movement, she flashed out in front of him. Through the open front door, I could see them going down the path to the road. The young husband had snatched up a heavy canvas bag of tools from which a hammer-handle stuck out at the top.

It was a beautiful spring morning, just as the young husband had said. At that time, there stood in front of the house a very old crab-apple tree. Are you acquainted with crab-apple trees in age, I wonder? Do you know their spring blooming which, May after May, makes a wild, riotous celebration of new life all over its high-held spreading crown of ancient branches? It is not only riotous to the eye with the rosy flame of uncountable blossoms, but to the ear, too, for it is all full of bees, frantic with springtime joy, humming and buzzing their sonorous way from flower to flower till the tall, old tree sounds like a deep cello string thrumming in the warm air.

That front-yard tree was perhaps a century old then. The young husband and wife were halted by the invisible gust of perfume dropping from it, and for a moment stopped to look up into its branches. The low, delicate thunder-throbbing of the bees came through the door into the room where I sat, the room so filled with the soap-and-water prose of house-keeping.

It was not two seconds, I suppose, as the clock ticks off time, that they stood there thus, looking up with exalted young faces blooming with rosy life. As they looked, they felt for each other's hands, as if to share in the flesh this moment of their united life.

There they have stood, in the glory of youth and of young love, ever since. I grew old and gray, they became mature, grew old, died, leaving behind them a memory of plain, country success in marriage and parenthood like many another. But to me, not like many another.

They went on, then, that morning, out of the gate, and turned up the road towards the mountain. They were not exactly skipping, for they were both grown up—just barely grown up—but their elastic step soon took them out of sight.

Back in the room where I sat motionless, the scissors in my hand—paper dolls no longer seemed as interesting as before— one of the two old ladies knitting asked the other, "What was that he said about her horses? There aren't any horses around here."

The other one said, "Oh, didn't you ever hear that story?" Then she told it. This is the way I remember it:

In the early nineteenth century, there lived, three or four farms down the valley road, a skillful, hard-working, successful farmer, who was bringing his son up in his own competent, practical ways. When the son was a young man, perhaps twenty, his father spent the free time in the early spring before serious farm-work began showing him how to train a pair of colts, wild, rebellious younger-generation horses, to develop into steady, useful, obedient work-horses. In those days it was serious business to train young horses. Success in farming depended on them. There were few machines, you see. The father was a master-hand at breaking colts, and loved this part of the work. It took a conscientious effort for him to turn over to his son this responsible and interesting part of his profession. But experience of life had turned him into a good teacher. He knew well enough that his son must learn and that he could not learn without being allowed to take on real responsibility. But how earnestly he impressed upon his son that responsibility is a mighty matter.

One morning they were going down to the meadow beside the river—our deep, cold, black river—to try out the horses with the mowing machine, always a dramatic moment in a horse's development. The younger man held the reins. But the older man walked close behind. The river, almost in spring flood, ran more formidable, blacker, deeper, more sinister than usual. The horses, their nerves on edge with the new clatter of the mowing machine at their heels, curvetted, stepped high, tossed their heads. But the well-taught younger man knew he mustn't let them run away, or get to kicking, or tangled up with the traces or anything. Everybody on a farm in those days knew how young horses never get over one really excited spell if they lose their heads. They lose their heads easily, too, young horses do. The farmer's son knew how important it was for him to do just the right thing. And he did. He held the reins tightly but not too tightly, speaking to the fractious young animals continuously in a special voice half-reassuring, half-peremptory, to which nervous horses, half-reassured, half-intimidated, respond by obedience.

"He was all taken up with those horses," said my aunt, who was telling the story, "so set on doing exactly the right thing with them that he never noticed where his father was.

"And then all of a sudden, he heard his father holler out, 'Help! Help!' from somewhere quite near. He didn't dare turn his head from the horses, but out of the side of his eye he saw that his father had fallen into the river. The old man had gone down and as he came up to the top, he screamed out, 'Help!' in a terrible scared voice. For he didn't know how to swim. Lots of farmers in the old days didn't—I suppose they couldn't take time to learn, they had so much work to do.

"Well, there he was, the son, holding the reins on those young horses that he'd been working with all winter, just at the minute when he was left alone with them in a tight spot.

"His father went down, again, with a dreadful scream which scared the horses. They began to rear and plunge and push each other sideways. The young farmer held to the reins for dear life; and when his father came up the second time, yelling, 'Help! Come help!' he shouted back, 'Can't leave my horses! Can't leave my horses!'"

The other woman laughed appreciatively. My aunt held up her knitting to look at it. Apparently they thought that was the end! I dropped my scissors and called out anxiously, "What happened? Did the farmer drown? Did the horses run away?"

My aunt said comfortably, "Oh, the story never said anything about that. That wa'n't the point."

Nor did I ever hear—and so I can't tell you—what was the literal end of that story. Nobody ever explained it to me. Looking back now, it seems to me that my elders took an especial pleasure in not explaining the point of these old-time stories. Perhaps they had a pre-Dewey divination that children would get the point better if they thought it out themselves.

Yet in the case of this particular story—although I assume that I have always grasped what the point was to the people who told it—for me, quite another aura hung around it. This was connected, as such indefinable associations often are, with one particular spot, and one particular sensory impression. For Proust, a moment of his childhood rose up before him whole and living with the taste of that little madeleine cake. For me, the association with this story of farmers and hayfields and farmers' horses always springs up when I pass the place where the old crab-apple tree stood.

Like the owners of the house who had been so young, it grew old, and after more than a century, it grew decrepit. Big branches fell off of it with every windstorm. Standing in the front yard as it did, everyone who went down the front path passed under it. Like other living things which in their prime had been up-surging fountains of beauty, it became a danger. Finally it was cut down, after a big wind had split it in two, clean to the root.

Not quite down. A stump was left to serve as feeding-station for the birds which had always fluttered in and out of the branches when they had stood tall and strong. Nobody had even especially noticed the crab-apple tree. They are not unusual in our valley. No one thought at all of the stump which, as I grew old in my turn, was the only visible trace left.

But I did. While it still stood, lifting its beautiful crown of incongruously useful blooms in the springtime, the bees humming in a fury of joy in its blossoms, I never passed it without stopping for a moment to look and listen, and to see again the young couple standing under it so long ago, hand in hand, in order to share in the flesh the impression of beauty and bloom and springtime of which they were a part.

They themselves had children, did their best with them, as most parents do, had all sorts of difficulties and all kinds of joys, did not always get on perfectly with each other, but always in the end, each reached for the other's hand, so that they went on sharing life until they died, very old people, leaving behind grown-up successful sons and daughters. You see, at the time I first heard that story, they were much older than I, although they really were so young. They were quite old when I was only middle-aged. Now they have been dead for years and forgotten. Except that I don't forget them.

Sometimes, now, out for a brief walk, leaning on my old lady's walking stick, perhaps with the thermometer well below zero, perhaps in the summer heat, I stop for a moment to look at the stump of the old tree. As I gaze dreamily at it, sometimes a near-by younger person says wonderingly, "Whatever are you looking at, Aunt Dorothy?" or, "Granny, what do you see in that old stump?"

Well, one thing I don't see is the "point" which that story has had for everybody else who has heard it. I still hear that "point" invoked once in a while when somebody sees a housemate so held by dust on furniture or distracted by weeds in the corn field as not to notice a sunset or a dawn. I know what is meant when a voice says in negligent irony, "Can't leave your horses, can you?"

That's a good point for any story to have. I'm in accord with it. But long ago, my imagination was shunted off on another set of rails when, as a little girl, who had never thought, one way or the other, about ever being married herself, I saw the young husband and wife standing close to each other, almost visibly drawn up to share the drunken ecstasy of springtime youth, but together, hand in hand. It was then that, for the first time, I thought hazily, It might be sort of nice to get married—sometime.

Before Adult Education
Was Thought of

John Conroy was one of the "characters" in the old Vermont village where I spent a good deal of my little girlhood. He was born so long ago, in the first half of the nineteenth century, that, in his youth, there was no classroom education open to him more liberal than learning to read and write and figure in the overcrowded village school. As he grew up, it was plain that he had a powerful, original mind. Most Arlington people recognized his native intelligence, but considered him "half-baked." And they were right. For lack of intellectual discipline and of wide information, his fine mind never functioned as it should. He didn't know what now any high-school graduate knows, something of what had been thought out in centuries before our times, and his reasoning was often not sound. He jumped ardently to ideas and conclusions which were new to him, but which acquaintance with history, or science, or economics would have shown him to be impractical and one-sided.

But he was born much more of an artist than an intellectual. His passion was music. In the restricted rural life of his boyhood there was no way for him to receive any musical training or even ever to hear good music. He learned to fiddle untaught. He was no dance fiddler, and indeed never played for a dance in his life. The music he wanted was the very finest. This austerely classical taste was, in itself, enough in those days to have him dubbed a very queer character indeed.

I realize now what didn't occur to me till much later—that such a love for Beethoven and Haydn and Bach and such a great distaste for trivial music was really so odd in a district-school-educated house-painter and isolated villager as to be inexplicable, without some influence in his earlier life of which I didn't know. Did he encounter in his boyhood and youth somebody with sound musical training? Maybe. I never heard anyone mention such a contact, or give any other explanation. But that proves nothing. I may have heard such a mention and remember not a word of it. For when I first remember John Conroy I was a little girl, perhaps ten years old, beginning to play the violin, and I took him for granted, just as he was, as ten-year-olds take everybody around them for granted.

I certainly took for granted my Aunt Mattie Canfield. In the world where John Conroy was first violin and I was second, Aunt Mattie was piano. She played that instrument as young ladies did in those days. Not that she was then a young lady; she was, like many stout middle-aged women in the 1880's, just a young lady grown old, having studied music like any other of the parlor "accomplishments," all learned by rote. But she had considerable facility, read music fluently, had a feeling for rhythm unshakeable as Red Mountain, and was always ready to do anything which might give pleasure.

In the front parlor of the Brick House, now the Community House, which was then my great-grandmother's house, we three used to have wonderful evenings. John Conroy was strongly inclined to ideas which people then considered radical —they would be called merely liberal now. And he lived up to his ideas in some odd ways. He objected rather belligerently to outward signs of social position, and would never wear a necktie, because he thought that was used to mark a difference between wage-earning people and those who didn't work for their living. But he always looked clean with a stiff, starched, white wing-collar, the sizable gold-plated shirt-stud gleaming baldly in front. Since we were used to it, we never thought it looked queer. Visitors to town did.

By that time of his life he had acquired a fine collection of violin music, quartets, trios, duets, his especial love being for strings playing together. He never liked singing, and always avoided the social gatherings around the piano to sing hymns, patriotic songs or the popular tunes of the day, which satisfied the mild taste for music of the people around him. We elders often think, we who still remember John Conroy before he was an eccentric old man, how he would have enjoyed, if he could have heard them before his ears became dulled by age, our modern record-players, with the beautiful chamber music which they pour into our homes.

Together we three, my dear Aunt Mattie pounding energetically at the piano, John Conroy as first violin, and I, my feet dangling far from the floor, as second violin, read music —page after page, if the notes were within our abilities, phrase after phrase when it was hard. That was the set-up for several evenings every week. We were happily engrossed by it, and as there was nobody around to hear us, except people passing by on the sidewalk in front of the house, it didn't trouble other folks.

Those evenings in my little girlhood, and later in my 'teens, opened music to me. For, like Aunt Mattie a generation before, I was "taking music lessons" as ordinary little girls did, sixty-five years ago. This meant that I was given scales and exercises for work and tuneful little "pieces" for pleasure. These had a shallow prettiness which had been worn to shreds by the time I had practiced enough to play the notes to my teacher's satisfaction. They had nothing at all in common with the breath-taking adventure of plunging into the deep waters of real music and swimming for dear life, going under at times—"Oh, John, where *are* you now?"—but coming to the surface at the indication he gave, and striking out again.

What did we read? Whatever was on the big sheets which John Conroy brought in and set on our music-stands. The first I remember well was Haydn, for whom as a child I came to have a fond, enchanted affection like that for a favorite, playful, fun-loving uncle. But there is a great deal to Haydn beyond his folk-fun, and John Conroy kept us insensibly advancing till we occasionally found ourselves stirred and exalted as by nothing else in our everyday lives. I must confess, too, that we read pages, or passages, sometimes only a few meaningful bars such as we could manage, out of a special (I'll say it was special!) "arrangement" for two violins and piano of the Beethoven symphonies. Yes, really. This is not a misprint. The orchestral "effects" in this arrangement were given to the piano. How my mild aunt, who had never in her life thundered or flashed fire, reveled in the loud rolling bass passages where she emerged from being piano and became drums! What good times we had, all of us!

By the time I was in the middle of my 'teens (and of course playing a little better), Beethoven was like another uncle, as familiar a voice and presence as Haydn but a presence bringing an awed, respectful attentiveness.

Any Bach? Yes, his voice was always heard at least once in each of these exciting, absurd, never-to-be-forgotten evenings in the front parlor. For a long time I thought that I didn't "like" Bach, and that I couldn't make sense out of anything but the shortest phrases. I thought I struggled my way through those endless twiddles only because John Conroy set the page up before me. Yet there was something odd—I noticed this early—as long as Bach was being played, I couldn't stop listening. And as I grew into my 'teens, I don't need to tell you what this unwilling fascination grew into.

And we read some Boccherini and some other eighteenth-century pages. The sounds we made must have been grotesque beyond imagining. With every note I was advancing into a world of pure and lasting joy.

At this point I perceive that I've forgotten to tell you that, barred by circumstance from the kind of life in which he would have developed freely, John Conroy drank too much. At times. Everybody knew this, even the ten-year-old child who waveringly played second violin to his first. But nobody minded, not even kind "Miss Mattie," brought up with decorous Victorian standards though she was. Nobody I knew laughed maliciously about his weakness, nor put on self-righteous reproving airs, nor called him (in my hearing) by the ugly name of drunkard. He never appeared for music when he was under the influence—not once—and so, I gathered through my pores, it was really no affair of ours.

But, of course, as the years went by, it became plain that we were all three on diverging roads—the old young lady who was my lovable aunt, the frustrated artist, the growing-up girl.

John Conroy lived, alone, in a one-story, long, one-roomed building on School Street. He began to grow somewhat deaf, his fingers stiffened with age and arthritis. I grew up, my ears gave out in the early deafness which ended my music-making, I was away at college, abroad, married, had children. Aunt Mattie died.

House-painting by day and playing his violin at night beside a wood-burning stove, John Conroy lived quite alone in the one big room of the battered old building. (It had been, so I've always heard, the Baptist church, in the first years of the nineteenth century, until there were no more Baptists in town.)

One summer when I came back from college, I remember his telling me that he had played his way, during the winter, through the Beethoven quartets—mighty compositions of which he could get only the faintest echo, as, inexpertly, pitifully, valiantly, he played his single violin part. The older members of his family died, the younger ones lived elsewhere, had other interests, John Conroy became "queerer" all the time. Now, just as he had always refused to wear a necktie, he refused to shave more than in the old-time farmer's schedule of once a week. His dimming hearing and his dwindling vitality silenced his violin. He was an old "character," of whom few people knew more than that he had odd ideas.

Towards the end of his life, his neighbors up and down School Street began to be concerned about the ancient solitary for fear he might not bother to get himself enough to eat. For, natural artist that he was, he felt the comforts of life to be unimportant. The kind housewives on his street would have been glad to invite the battered, shabby, rather frowsy old workingman to share their meals with them off and on, when he liked. But they didn't try this, for he had become cross-grained in his old age, and couldn't abide the idea of sitting down at the table with other people. He had lived alone too many years for that. And he had never liked what is called sociable chat. His gingham-clad neighbors forbore any attempt to reason with him. Middle-aged young matrons as they were, they knew as little of what John Conroy had been, as of what he might have become. To them he was just a crochety, notional old man. But in their code of neighborliness, crochety old age had its own right. Those warm-hearted women put their heads together to devise some arrangement to help him, suited to his "character." They invented this plan: they set aside for him one compartment of their iceboxes. In this they always kept food of the kind everybody eats—a piece of pie, some cold meat, some fruit, a slice of freshly baked cake, some beans—part of whatever was on their own tables. Their doors were never locked, and, late or early, as the notion took him, John Conroy stepped into the kitchen and helped himself. The head of the family, sleeping upstairs, heard—perhaps at one o'clock in the morning—somebody stirring in the kitchen, thought, John coming for his supper, turned over and went to sleep again. Or a newcomer to Arlington making a call in the front parlor might say warningly to her hostess, "I see rather a rough-looking old man coming up on your back porch." To which the hostess, after a hasty glance out of the window, would say, "It's all right. John Conroy coming for his lunch."

They made no good-sense, heavy-handed effort, natural though this would have seemed, to argue with the strange old man, or to dictate to him a sensible, regular way of life which would have suited them but not him. They left a margin around him in which he breathed freely to the end of his life, up to his eightieth year.

This gentleness for the frustrated old artist, this kindness, generous, imaginative, delicate, self-effacing, seemed to me as truly poetry as any I ever read in words.

Christmas in Arlington

Introductory Note:
Ourselves As Seen From Paris

The following description about the way in which Christmas is celebrated in my home town was brought out by a request coming from Paris. The editor of a French magazine asked me for an account of the "local customs at Christmas in an American village."

At first, I was inclined to reply that we had no special "local customs," but on second thought wrote out with quite liberal accuracy just what does go on in Arlington at Christmas. I have been struck by two contrasting reactions to it. The Paris editor's reception of this photographic, unornamented snapshot of our Christmas "customs" was a charmed astonishment. "Here is a corner of America, obviously authentically presented, which is amazingly different from the stereotyped picture familiar to Europeans from other descriptions of life in the U.S.A., with gangsters, Hollywood glitter, and millionaires sunning on Florida beaches."

Vermonters who have read it have laid the paper down with the remark, "Well, it's all right, but I don't see anything especially *interesting* in it. Every Vermont town does something like this. Who would have thought of writing it out in French for French readers?"

These two impressions have met in our minds with a shock of contrast and incomprehension—"How odd! What a strange idea—!" Little by little they settle down to some sort of unified idea, and we are now saying to each other, "Well—! Maybe a person would better sprinkle a lot of the salt of cautiousness over what gets told to us about the life of other folks—in Africa, in Indonesia, in Iceland—maybe there's a mix-up of things that don't belong together at all, such as imagining that life in an American village or small town ever has any color at all reflected from Hollywood, gangsters and millionaires."

We rub our eyes and look more closely at world reporting.

Our village of Arlington, Vermont, is a small old settlement, which was founded in 1764 by young people coming up through the untracked woods from western Connecticut, to the south of us in New England. They brought with them a spirit of cheerful enjoyment of community life which has persisted to this day, almost two hundred years later. The community is small, numbering about fourteen hundred people —the same number (within three or four) as at the time of the American Revolution at the end of the eighteenth century.

At first the only church was the Anglican church, and this still—an old stone building with a tower high among the tall trees which now shade the village street—is a landmark and monument as well as a church from which innumerable baptismal processions, and weddings and funerals have issued as the human life in the town renews itself.

Like most small communities set in mountain country, the population is divided geographically into villages, which used to be more separated in spirit than since good roads and automobiles bring the towns' children all together fraternally in one central school. The old Congregational church is the one attended by many of the people in these smaller divisions of our already small Arlington.

In the late 1840's people of another nationality began to appear, the Irish, Roman Catholics, came in as workers on the new railroad. They have become an integral element of our community, Americans, with whom life is shared in amity, with comradely feeling.

This background gives an idea of the reasons which lie behind the Christmas celebration here in which all the various kinds of people join with hearty good will.

The beginning is always a Christmas evening at the public school—in America the public school is, almost without exception, a part of the life of almost every family with children. The Christmas program is one in which the children especially delight. Each class in the school from little ones on up to the older ones presents some one feature of the long evening to which all the parents and friendly townspeople come, delighting in seeing the emergence from babyhood and the kindergarten age of those who are to be our future comrades and fellow-citizens. The younger children give a little Christmas play, or symbolic dance, or song. The older children always present a *tableau vivant* of the traditional Christmas scene, the baby in the manger in the stable, the three Wise Men in adoration, with everybody at the end, including the audience, singing some of the well-known Christmas songs like the "O come, let us adore Him." Nearly everyone in the audience, you see, has been a child, helping to present on that very stage the tableau.

On the main village street the two churches stand, on one side, the older stone church of St. James, which is the Anglican church, and on the other side the well-cared-for Roman Catholic church of St. Columban, which is as much a part of the community by this time, after a century, as the mountains around our town. Children from both churches and from every outlying settlement gather there on the Sunday before Christmas, to sing carols, around a spruce tree, tall and dark in the snow, which was planted in memory of an elderly citizen who gave the years of his retirement to serving the community. "Dr. Kent's tree," it is called, and around it gather not only the children but their families with them. The old Christmas carols which are sung there are known to you in France, little children learning them by hearing them sung by the grown-ups. The chimes in the church tower play the Christmas carols, too, in the intervals of singing. Sometimes, as last year, one of the winter snows begins in the midst of this outdoor singing, the large white flakes slowly drifting down, the children delighted to see them, this white veil adding a touch of poetry to the rustic scene.

Both the Roman Catholic priest and the clergyman of the Anglican church come and go in this "community sing," as it is called.

Across the street stands the old Community House, which was given the town by a member of one of the founding families of Arlington. It belongs to everybody, for every variety of meeting, and after the Christmas "community sing," everybody troops across the street together, fathers and mothers and children, to little cakes and hot cocoa, and coffee for the grown-ups. This makes a delightfully sociable ending to the outdoor singing in what is now the winter-dark night, the light from the windows yellow across the snow.

The session of the school always ends a little while before Christmas, and in those days the whole community, especially the children of course (for it is the children's great festival), is busy with all sorts of Christmas preparations. The children are allowed in the kitchen to make all sorts of things, cookies and homemade candy, which they take to older people who are ill, or just too old and feeble to get out to any community celebration. This neighborly attention is an important part of the Christmas celebration for each church (Roman Catholic, Congregational, Anglican). Baskets filled with specially good things to eat—many of them homemade—and gay with bright Christmas decoration, are carried by friends to the sick, the very old, the house-bound, with cheerful Christmas greetings. And of course there are groups who go from house to house singing carols.

This is a really lovely event for each child. The little ones, too young really to sing, go along with the older ones and a few mothers or teachers or aunts who drive the cars to take them far out into the country. In the village they just walk from house to house, standing outside the lighted windows (for hardly anybody in America, at least in the country, ever closes the windows with curtains against the outside world, but leaves them open, bright, cheerful squares of yellow light shining out over the snow). All the children and the few elders with them group themselves and just begin to sing. You in France probably know what they sing, *"Noël, Noël,"* or the English version of *"Ce matin, j'ai rencontré le train,"* or *"Adeste fideles,"* or the innumerable English carols like "O little town of Bethlehem," or "Hark, the herald angels sing"—the same Christmas songs which were sung long ago and have never been forgotten in this static old community.

The people in the house (now that I am quite old myself, near to eighty, I know what the people in the house do, although I used of course, in the older days, to go out with groups of children) gather around the window, sitting quietly by the warm fire in their own living rooms, listening with delight to the fresh young voices coming from the children they can't see at all for all the light is in the house, of course. All the old people have something ready to take or send out to the children as they turn away—little homemade cakes, or candy, or perhaps nothing but a hearty call through an open door of "Thank you, children, thank you!"

And of course in each church, midnight Mass is celebrated or a midnight candlelight service. The children often don't go to that, for it's too late for them. They stay at home with an aunt or a grandmother while their parents are in their pews. The children fall asleep, lapsing from the happy, friendly atmosphere of communal rejoicing in which they have been for the last few days into sleep, with the sound of Christmas carols dropping down from the church tower through the snow.

Ann Eliza

When I was a child, it used to seem to me that Arlington older people kept in their memories a sort of invisible show-case, on the shelves of which stood row upon row of varying specimens of human nature. A great-uncle might say casually laying down the evening newspaper, "A lot of Ann Eliza Bascomb in that, today." From his gray-haired sister knitting at the other side of the hearth fire came a murmured exclamation, "I was thinking of Ann Eliza this very morning. D'ye know it must be forty years since she died!"

If the face of a listening child was lifted towards them in inquiry, Ann Eliza would be taken down from that invisible shelf, dusted off and held up to view.

The first look at her was this story: Seeing a younger neighbor passing the house, going up to the "center of town"— that is, the post office, the store, the church, the doctor's house —Ann Eliza called out to her, "Stop in on your way home, will ye, and tell me the news from town."

So on her way back the younger woman stopped and, leaning over the railing of the front porch, said, "Since you reminded me, I listened and asked questions and I have a lot of news."

The older woman settled herself in her rocking chair and said, eagerly, "Let's hear."

The younger woman began. "Lucy Bracket has finally got around to deciding what kind of a wedding she'll have—not at home, after all she's said. In church. And she's going to have *his* sister to stand up with her. And Jim Edgerton said in the post office that he's made more syrup this year out of his sugarbush than...."

Ann Eliza's face had been clouding. She now cried out in exasperation, "Oh, I don't mean *that* kind of news! *Who's sick?*"

After the pause for a laugh, Ann Eliza was turned to show another side. "D'ye remember how she was as she got older? Seems as though the only thing she wanted to think about was what people had done that was wrong. She'd talk her way up and down the street, one house after another—such stories! One man had taken money from the Sunday School collection, such a woman took morphine on the sly, in the next house they were all whiskey-topers, down the street farther the woman of the house was getting ready to run away with the hired man! One day, I remember, I'd listened to her carrying on like that, and thought I'd try to make her see how she sounded. I said to her, 'Ann Eliza, don't you think it's queer that in a whole town there aren't *any* decent families—not one?' I thought she'd burst out laughing. But she never cracked a smile. She thought for a moment. Then she said, just as serious, 'Why, yes, it *is* queer! I never thought of it before. Now I do, I'm astonished. But there isn't one of them that isn't an Indian!' "

Of course the listening child asked, puzzled, "What did she mean—'Indian'?"

She was seldom given an explicit answer to her questions.

"What d'ye *think?* You don't s'pose she meant it as a compliment, do you?"

The old voices went on. "D'ye remember how, after a while, it got so that when somebody passed along a piece of news, he was asked at once, 'Who told you that?' And if he said, 'Ann Eliza Bascomb,' they just said, 'Oh—' and started talking about something else.

"I remember how folks, even people new to town, finally didn't go in to see her any more, hardly ever. She'd sit there on her front porch, all alone. And they'd walk by, sort of fast as if they had business on hand. Maybe they'd nod to her, and call out, 'Fine day, isn't it?' But they didn't stop. Everybody knew beforehand what she would talk about, if they did.

"Once she sent word to me, special, to go to see her and help her with a door that wouldn't shut. I did and got it fixed. As I was going away, she said, half-mad at everybody, half-sorry for herself, 'Niram, what's the matter with people in this town? You're the first person in three weeks to step foot inside my house! What ever in this world have I done to make them act so?' "

The great-aunt laid down her knitting to exclaim, "She *did?* I never knew that. What d'ye say to her?"

The old man took up his newspaper again. From behind it his voice was noncommittal. "I didn't say anything. It was too late to say anything then."

The Corkscrew

"I cannot tell what the truth may be,
     But this is the tale as 'twas told to me."

To be accurate, the tale never was told ... at least not completely. The following is what I have pieced together about it from much questioning, and not a little use of imagination to clear up points which no one seemed to remember exactly, but which must have been more or less as I intend to write them ... or else none of the rest of it makes any sense at all.

My interest in this fragment of town history was first aroused over forty years ago, as I was watching a line of the privileged sex (women were still second-class citizens then) moving towards the ballot box to vote for or against the building of a new school. As he shuffled past me I heard one old gray-beard muttering, "I ain't a-goin' to vote to bond the town." Apparently others agreed with him. The new school was not voted that year. I set myself to find out why.

For the beginning we must go 'way back into the nineteenth century, when a railroad—any railroad—was thought of as a perpetual fountain of easy money. The public rushed to buy shares with the same guileless enthusiasm it felt later for oil-wells ... now for uranium deposits ... and centuries ago, in Holland, for prize tulip bulbs. Everybody was sure there was big money in railroads. So there was ... for those who knew how to get it. Wasn't one of the great fortunes in those days started by a stock speculator and his friends who got temporary working majority control of a line, then profitable, who plastered it with new bonds, squeezed it dry and unloaded their stock on the public just before the crash? Hard on the public? Yes. How many small savings-bank accounts were drawn out and used to buy gaudily engraved certificates —six shares in Amalgamated Union ... five in Consolidated Traction ... and so on—carefully preserved, hoping against hope, through needy old age; and, after the funeral, listed by a cynical executor as "Of no value except to paper a room with!" Oh, well, "There's a sucker born every minute!" *"Caveat emptor*— let the buyer look out for himself." The big fish had no time to worry about the fate of the small fry. They had troubles of their own. For this was also the time of no-holds-barred, biting-and-gouging brawls between big tycoons, with no Interstate Commerce Commission to police the fight.

Along with all the rest of our nation, our small Vermont town was all but skinned alive financially in the process of securing railroad transportation in the mid-nineteenth century. I can't claim anything unique in the general story of this fleecing of naïve country folks. But some of the details as to how the deal was put over on a whole community may differ from the details of the contacts between your own home town and the speculators in railroad financing. And of course it is a truism to say that what happens to you is not so vital an influence on your life as the way you take it. The way Arlington took it, that's the story I'm setting down here.

At first the town, like a man sandbagged from ambush, did not understand, not at all, not in the least, what was happening, what had happened. If you find the outline-sketch of the deal which follows in the next few paragraphs confused and confusing, you'll know how it looked to the people of a small, rural, mountain township.

In the late 1840's, a group of capitalists built a railroad through the western valley of Vermont. At least I suppose it was a group. We used to lay our misfortunes to a single man, but it is now my guess that he was probably only the mouthpiece for others cleverer, more powerful than he. The only drawback to this railroad was that it ended close to Vermont's southern border. Beyond that point, any through freight it carried would have to be routed over the tracks of another company...to avoid libel suits, let's call it the "Seaboard and Western." This pattern was usual enough in those days all over the United States, before little scraps of trackage were knit together into imposing transcontinental systems. But in this case there was a hitch. The "Seaboard and Western" charged an impossibly high rate for picking up and carrying to its final destination all freight which came to it over the Vermont line. The new line of tracks down our valley was blocked. The door was slammed shut for all towns lying on the line of tracks. All that Americans hoped for from railroads in the mid-nineteenth century, they had joyfully seen coming to them—access to hugely larger markets for what they had to sell, and what they had to buy being brought to them more rapidly and at much lower prices.

But they were told that the slammed door could be opened. How? By money. An extension of the new tracks could be built—a mere fifty or sixty miles—till the Vermont railroad connected directly with the great Midland Railroad (not its real name).

How could money be found for such an extension, by mountain towns with no surplus cash, and no revenue except yearly taxes paid by people who worked hard for their livings? The one way was, of course, for the Towns to borrow the sum needed—its thousands and thousands and thousands of dollars seemed enormous to Vermonters. But they were told, and this statement turned out factually accurate, any big city bank would loan that huge sum to a group of Vermont Towns, if their Town Meetings would vote to instruct their elected Town officials to sign some printed papers called bonds, each one obligating the Town to make moderate-sized repayments of the money borrowed, year by year, and of course to pay interest. The bank would sell these bonds to individuals—to "careful investors who prefer a *sure* thing to what is called a good thing." Who would own the fifty- or sixty-mile tracks of this vital extension? Why, the Towns which had paid for it, of course. Every cent of profit from its use would come into the Treasuries of the Towns which were to be absolute owners of a profitable railroad.

Of course, the proposition was discussed—with desperate seriousness by the farmers, and store-keepers, and doctors, and blacksmiths, and clergymen, and marble-cutters and saw-mill operators who make up Town Meetings. Every voting citizen, almost without exception, had gone through district school, some through local Academies or Seminaries, a few were college graduates. Hardly one was illiterate. But very few had had any experience with the modern way of financing the building of the new modern invention of the railroad.

There was some opposition to the proposal—cooler, usually gray-haired heads, cautious or timid men, a few thick-skulls who could not at all understand what the plan meant. But Town Meeting decisions are taken by a majority of votes. In the end, the majority voted for what looked like "progress," and business initiative. Bonding themselves to repay in the future, all the Towns concerned borrowed the money. With what the Towns paid in for their allotments, the rails were laid, the new line was ready to operate. It had a name of its own (now forgotten). Its wavy layout gave it a folk-name, "The Corkscrew."

What do you suppose happened next? Does it surprise you to learn that the "Seaboard and Western" saw the light? Always anxious for extra business, it at once cut its charge for transfer and trackage so low that practically all through freight for the south and west handled by the Vermont railroad could be, and from now on was, routed through the "Seaboard and Western" instead of over the meandering Corkscrew. The Corkscrew did not have nearly enough local freight along its line to make both ends meet without the through traffic. This was now carried over the tracks of the "Seaboard and Western" which had formerly refused it. The railroad "owned" by the Towns went into bankruptcy. After the privileged debts were paid, the Towns got no money to speak of in return for the sums they had put into it. At the bankruptcy sale, the Vermont railroad picked up the Corkscrew property for almost nothing. After that, they gave it enough through freight to keep up the track and pay running expenses, only a slight burden because all capital amortization charges had been wiped out.

As for the Towns . . . well, the trains kept running on the Vermont railroad and that was what the Towns had wanted. True. But after a while, looking around them at similar cases in neighboring states, our voters (all of them newspaper readers) woke up to the fact that if they had only sat tight, some sort of compromise would certainly have been worked out between the two groups of money-boys. Maybe the "Seaboard and Western" crowd, or maybe the Vermont railroad crowd, would have won in the poker game. In every poker game somebody loses; in this transaction the loser would have been a group of rich people who would have lost some of their money, not poor tax-payers in poor mountain towns. *But the trains would have run. The tracks already laid would not have rusted.*

The Towns were stuck with a staggering load of bonds, and with accruing interest, adding up, before the transaction was finally ended years later, to more than twice the original loan . . . all of which the people of the Towns would have to pay.

Or *did* they have to? I don't know exactly what happened in the other Towns involved. In Arlington the matter was debated in the livery stable, in the general store, in farmhouse kitchens, on the steps of the tavern, wherever men of voting age foregathered. Some argued that the job was an obvious frame-up, that no court would decide against the Towns. Or, if the verdict went the other way, what could the bondholders do about collecting? "If they want to levy on our Town Hall, let 'em. That's the only real estate the Town owns. We can get along without it all right. We can hold our meetings in the church."

"Or do you suppose they could freeze the taxes as the Town Treasurer collects them?" A fearful possibility that—brushed aside with a show of bravado.

"Oh well, if we hire a foxy lawyer he can find ways of putting them off time and again ... till they get sick and tired of it, and write the whole thing off as a bad debt. That's what speculators often do!"

Years went by, filled with these discussions. What was at issue stood blackly in the foreground of all planning for the future—everybody's individual future, the Town's future in which every one of us had a share.

The interest on our debt was voted groaningly at every year's Town Meeting. But no decision about the whole debt was made, every discussion ended in the postponement of a vote. Waves of wish-thinking kept churning up the minds and hearts of the citizens of our little, country, back-roads community.

But like actual waves, all their sound and fury, foam and spray unavailing, they dashed against and fell back from a granite shore-line. Call it what you will—crack-brained idealism, the dead hand of ancestral tradition, or just honesty, undramatic, unpicturesque—the conviction grew that, whether you said the voters had made fools of themselves, or had been taken in by sharpers, no matter how you twisted the story, you couldn't get around the fact that *now* those bonds were owned by plain people just like us, who had given up their own good money to buy them, trusting to our promise to pay them back in full when the bonds fell due.

I don't apologize for making the above account so sketchy. When I was a girl, the older generation agreed that, in its main outline, the affair took place as I am reporting it. Like all elderly story-tellers, they differed widely on details. But for us today the main question is not just How—or When or Who said What. Here, as always, what happens to you doesn't begin to be as important as the way you take it. And how my town took it does not rest on hearsay. From now on, the story—plain and clear—can be dug from laconic entries in those old Town Reports which lie dog-eared and dusty in every farm attic.

Arlington took its hard luck standing up. "The other Towns can decide as they see fit. For us a debt's a debt, no matter how contracted." Year by year, in little driblets, bond after bond with full interest was repaid until at last every one of them had been paid off. The Town was free of debt. Those were proud years. They were also lean years ... lean beyond the imagination of moderns.

The splintered planking of the Elm Street bridge ought to be replaced, but . . . .

It would be nice to have a new carpet on the front stairs, before the daughter of the house had her wedding, but . . . .

"Mother, can I have the money to buy a new pair of galoshes? The old ones leak. My feet get soaking wet when it's thawy weather. . . ." Sadly answered, "No, I'm afraid not, Charley. Try to make the old ones do until we save up enough to pay our taxes."

So that was that. No, there was more to it. Whether we look back or forward, nobody can find a beginning or an end in the chain-reaction of cause and effect. Years went by. Efforts for better schools failed many times. But after a while, enough of the older generation had taken their bitter memories to the grave with them. Young voters, full of the rash courage of inexperience, had grown up. Finally architect's plans were drafted for the dream-school we had waited for all those years. The money was voted, a committee appointed to see on what terms, if any, we could borrow what seemed to us the immense sum we needed before the building contract could be let. Perhaps, we feared, no one would trust such a large sum to such a little country community, which had no material possessions for security beyond a rather battered, ancient Town Hall, its clapboards badly in need of new paint.

After a visit to the city the committee came back and made this report: "We started by trying to talk about our assessed valuation and our tax rate, but they wouldn't let us finish. One of those hard-boiled Boston bankers cut us short. 'Don't bother with all that,' he said. 'We've looked up your financial record. *You're a good risk*. Just tell us how much you need. We'll be glad to have you borrow it from us. We can sell your bonds for enough over par to shave the net interest you'll have to pay, down to about $1\frac{8}{10}$ per cent.'"

The Hen and the
Hired Man

The brick house on our Main Street, across the street from the Old Burying Ground of St. James Church, was home for my great-grandmother and assorted members of her family circle for many years. After her death, when it was still filled with elderly great-uncles and great-aunts and elderly cousins, it was my home, off and on, all through my childhood and youth. My father was a member of university faculties in various places, so that in the wintertime we lived here and there, something like a family of a Methodist minister who moves professionally from one place to another. But I was always sent back to Arlington for long summers, and often for sojourns in the winter when the family plans turned out that way.

There is a little room at the head of the front stairs. It is now used as a kitchen for one of the apartments rented to help pay the expenses of running the building as a Community House. In my childhood, it was my tiny bedroom, plenty big enough to be shelter-refuge for a little girl who never became at all a big person, even when grown up. There was nothing the least bit ornamental about that cell, just a cot bed, a chest of drawers, a washstand, and three or four hooks for clothes. It was its undefinable, protective atmosphere of "hands off" which endeared it to me. It was my very own. I loved having it always ready for me to step into this atmosphere, no matter how long or how short a time it had been since I was there before, nor how far away I had been.

You wouldn't think, would you, that a little room which faced out towards nothing but the old garden at the back of the house would be a viewpoint for observation of human life. But I remember two happenings which provided me with some of the raw material for understanding. But then, I suppose, everything that happens to youngsters is such raw material.

One day I had hooked my elbows over the rather high window sill and, reveling in the exquisite leisure of the young, was dreamily looking out into a beautiful early June morning. Nothing could have seemed more peaceful than that back yard. The Plymouth Rock hens, of which a flock was always kept up back of what is now the little apartment building, were mildly crooning as they stepped around over the fresh green grass. In the garden the hired man, John Robinson, was down on his knees, thinning out the young lettuce plants. He, too, was crooning happily; in his case this meant he was softly whistling: "Yankee Doodle." His hat was pushed to the back of his head; the black earth of the well-kept garden was opened to the sun and smelled warm and June-like.

As I idly watched the blandly tranquil scene, the cheerful

man and the contented hens, I noticed that, incautiously, John Robinson had left the gate to the garden open, so that there was a break in the picket fence which protected it from animals and poultry. I noticed, too, an elderly hen wandering in that direction. She saw the gate was open. She sauntered in and looked around her with beady, bright eyes. The well-cultivated, loose, loamy soil evidently looked like a good place to get angleworms. In a minute she was as hard at work as John Robinson and as happy, crooning to herself the equivalent in hen-language of his "Yankee Doodle." Just as instinct had told her, there were worms in that rich, black soil! With sweeping strokes of her long, sinewy legs she made that loam fly! Her strong claws drove deep into the radish bed. With every energetic scratch she upturned a worm and uprooted a healthy young radish plant.

For a little while, all was peaceful. The ecstatic hen and the happy hired man worked away at cross purposes with complete enjoyment, and I watched them as in a trance, wondering what would happen next.

Then John Robinson turned his head. When he saw that infernal fowl tearing up his radish bed, he was, for an instant, frozen in fury. Then he sprang to his feet, snatched his hat from his head, and yelling, *"Get out of here!"* he flung it at her with all his might.

It did not hit her, but fell close. She hadn't noticed that there was anybody else in the garden, and at this unexpected shock, she leaped high into the air, wings and legs outspread, with a scream as loud as John's yell. The hired man bellowed at her again, and started for her on the run, his great workshoes pounding across the carefully weeded lettuce bed. Flapping her wings and screeching, the terrified hen, squawking loudly, fled across the garden, the loose earth of the vegetable beds flying from under her claws.

But by that time she was hysterical and had quite forgotten the location of the gate. Half-flying, half-running, a wild swirl of fluttering feathers, she fetched up slam against a tight section of the picket fence.

Behind her lay a track of destruction in the seed beds. John Robinson was frantic at the sight of it. He bawled, "Get out of here," stooped, picked up his hat, and flung it at her again, this time with very good aim. It hit her full amidships. Struggling to get her balance she went into a series of leaps and squawks which were pyrotechnic. I had never seen a hen carry on like that, and since I was still young enough to be irresponsible about what happened in the adult world, I was absorbed by the spectacle.

John Robinson ran after the hen again, his roars of fury mingling with her screams. She fled from him at top speed—and of course since she was now beside herself, soon ran head on against the fence with its thickset pickets. Idiotic in panic, she thrust her head as far as it would go between two of the pickets, and squirmed and flapped wildly trying to force her body through. No go! She drew her head back, pushed it between the next two pickets, drew it back, thrust it between the next two, always squawking at the top of her voice. Thus she rocketed along, sticking her head between the slats, pulling it back, sticking it frantically through again. Every feather on her was awry. After her John pounded, throwing his hat at intervals, and shouting, "Get out of here, I say!" I don't need to tell you what the garden looked like after two or three minutes of this chase.

Then below my window, the back door of the brick house opened. My ancient great-aunt, Mary Ann Canfield, came out.

I saw her at once, for I looked straight down on the top of her sunbonneted head. But the crazed hen and the maddened hired man did not notice.

My great-aunt was then an enormously stout and very old woman. She had long ago given up any effort to keep her figure in shape with corsets, and nearly always wore a Mother Hubbard gingham apron which fell from her shelf-like bosom to the very ground. Decent women in those days never showed their feet. She wore the sunbonnet because decent women in those days always protected their complexions from the sun. From above I could not see her face; but from long acquaintance with her, I knew its expression—one she often wore, of cold contempt for human idiocy. Silently, as if on rollers, she moved forward towards the open garden gate.

Now John Robinson saw her. Evidently he knew, as well as I did (whether he could see it or not), what the expression on her face was. For he stopped short and hung his head.

Very slowly and without a sound she moved in through the open gate, and even more slowly up along the garden path, towards the hysterical hen, still spasmodically flapping her disheveled wings, wild-eyed, her voice almost gone, but occasionally emitting a hoarse squawk. When Aunt Mary was fairly close to the hen she stood perfectly motionless, a thick pillar of gingham. The hen, almost worn out, went on squawking and fluttering, but less and less. Finally her jerking wings fell to stillness, and she closed her beak.

Aunt Mary waited a minute or two longer, and then with a slow deliberate motion threw out one single grain of corn, one only. Then she waited again. The hen muttered a squawk, fluttered her feathers a little, looked all around uneasily, and then with a darting gesture of distrust picked up one grain of corn and swallowed it. Aunt Mary moved back one step only in the direction of the gate. She dropped another grain. Uncertainly, the hen moved forward and snatched up that grain. Then Aunt Mary moved back another step, waited a minute, and dropped another grain.

Thus leading the quieted hen, she backed herself very slowly out of the gate. The hen followed. When they were both outside, Aunt Mary shut the gate. Then she cast one look, just one, at the abashed John Robinson. I couldn't see her sunbonnet-shaded face, but I knew what the expression was.

If you think that this minutely small episode provided no food for thought during the growing-up years of the little girl who later became deeply concerned with the procedures of all kinds of education—well, you can just guess again.

Mais Où Habitent
les Paysans?

In the old days before the First World War, when no one
pestered you about passports or visas, when a second-class
return ticket cost little more than a hundred dollars, the
Fisher family enjoyed many a longish vacation in Europe.
Nothing strange about that. Other Americans had the tourist
habit. What was remarkable—and we could hardly believe the
news her letter brought us—was the sudden determination
of Céline Sibut, one of my most beloved, intimate, life-long
friends, to make the ocean crossing in reverse, to spend the
summer with us in our Arlington home.

You cannot possibly take in what this trip meant to her—
and to us—unless I set down at least an outline-sketch of her
background. She was an excellent and successful teacher in the
Paris public schools, a position earned through passing many
rigorous examinations in advanced academic education. She

was also a highly cultivated woman in the usual European meaning of that word. More than that, she was steeped to the marrow of her bones in the best "Age of Enlightenment" tradition. When she saw "Liberty, Equality, Fraternity!" carved, as it is, on French government buildings, her heart beat more briskly, she held her head higher. "Yes, that was as it should be!"

Her only regret was that progress towards complete, universal social democracy was so slow—that practice lagged so far behind lip-service. She had always been one of the French people who admire what we think of as the "American Idea" of social organization, and she hoped more and more from it as a leaven to European life. Unlike many women, as she grew older, she became more impatient with case-hardened conservatism.

And now she had come to Vermont, not only to renew her old friendship with us, but also to see with her own eyes how the "American Idea" was working out. We did our best to show her everything. Our ancient Model-T Ford rattled along the highway, along hilly side roads where the poor, smaller farms lay ... down again into a village in the valley ... up the next ridge in low speed, climbing another bumpy road with farmhouses strung along it. Occasionally, since of course we knew everybody we passed and they knew us, we stopped the car, got out and showed her the inner arrangements of a plain dairy barn, or stepped into a neighbor's house to let her see what an American Vermont farm kitchen looked like, with its wood-burning range, the running water piped to the sink for dishwashing.

Acting as interpreter, for she knew no English—this was in fact the first time she or any of her circle had set foot across the French frontier—it was often brought home to us what barriers stand in the way of understanding—of approaching close enough to conceive of a foreign way of life as possible, as actually followed by real live people.

My next-door neighbor, just down the hill from our house, was at that time an elderly Vermont farm woman who had scarcely ever been farther from Arlington than on her very occasional trips to the great metropolis of Bennington (population considerably under ten thousand) seventeen miles away to the south of us, our shire-town, and shopping center, which until the era of concrete roads, not even dreamed of at the time of Céline's visit, was almost as far from us because of rough, rutted, snow-filled or mud-mired roads as Korea from our grandchildren now. She was a great friend of the household and came at once to see "the lady from France." As she went out after a conversation in which I acted as two-way translator, she said with surprised and friendly accent, "Why, she's real nice, isn't she! I never see a nicer woman. Ain't it a pity she can't talk!"

Céline, on her side, made a comment almost as naïve as that of this simple daughter of Vermont, when she first drove with us down the Main Street of Arlington. In those days, people still sat on their front porches in the afternoon. Yes, try to imagine a time when there was no procession of automobiles whirring past with a mounting crescendo and decrescendo of noise as they flash into view and flash out again, when nothing moved along the street except an occasional horse-drawn wagon or buggy. Naturally, the front porch then was just about as intimately a part of the family home as the living room was. So, as we drove slowly along the street that afternoon, our French visitor saw whole families out on their front porches, older women sitting to mend or crochet or to read, the children playing on the sidewalk, somebody stepping out from the house with a pan of potatoes to peel, to enjoy the fresh air and family talk. As we passed along, Céline gazed at this living exhibition of Vermont life ... unmistakably like all family life everywhere ... with an expression which had in it as much astonishment as our old Vermont neighbor had felt when confronted with a foreign language. Presently she turned to me and said, "You can't imagine how strange it makes me feel to think of all these people having been here all these years, just living—and I never knew of their existence until now!" Although I found her remark a little vague, I guessed at the general trend of what she was trying to say. I did not press her to be more exact, since I could see that the idea was too new to her for a clearer statement.

We did not confine our sight-seeing to farms and kitchens. Always we did our conscientious best to think of everything in our valley which might possibly be of interest to her: schools, of course she took a special interest in them, as a teacher herself; churches, shops—such as they were; factories. When visiting these last we were especially careful to point out that such small woodworking establishments—all we had in Vermont—could by no means give her a notion of modern America. All our visitors from the big centers, so we warned her, insisted that Vermont was a tiny backwater—at least fifty years behind the rest of the United States and losing ground every minute.

We thought we had really covered what there was to see pretty well. Lots and lots of misconceptions had been ironed out, differences of opinion stated, accepted, smiled at without any hard feeling. For example, you may be interested to learn, she had been really horrified to find that we washed our dishes with *soap*. "Why, if I had known that, I wouldn't have been able to eat a mouthful! In France we always use washing soda for that. Soap leaves such a disgusting after-taste!" Her exclamation brought back to my mind a lecture I had received years before from a Parisian friend who insisted on the stomach-turning effect of soap used on tableware...even if you didn't know it had been used, you could taste it...anybody could...spoiling every mouthful of your next meal. Alas for the certainty of prejudices! Here was Céline, eating with relish, without a suspicion for many weeks, until she happened to notice that I was using the noxious product in my dish-washing. Something to be learned from that fact about human nature, don't you think?

One by one we had covered a great many items, and in our discussions Céline had picked up a good deal of our local history, as well as—so we thought—a pretty sound understanding of the sort of life going on around us. Then one evening just before her departure for home, she astonished us as, stirring with a quick movement in her chair, she lifted her head with a bright expression of curiosity and interest and asked, "But there is one thing you never have shown me, *où habitent les paysans?*—where do the peasants live?"

I invite you to meditate on the full meaning of that question. Remember that it did not come from a hard-and-fast believer in the beauty of unchanging caste lines. It came from a woman devoted to the brotherhood of man, ardently looking forward to a future when that brotherhood might be more accomplished. And yet all her past life had so fixed on her mind an acceptance of "the way things are" that even when she met it face to face she could not recognize that before her was a promise of "the way things might be." She had just not been able to imagine that the pleasant farmhouses we passed, with lawns and flowers around, could possibly be the home of people who actually did the work.

As we tried to make her see what was clear to us, we ourselves learned more about the life of peasants in France than we had ever guessed, although we had lived in France a good many times off and on. We looked deeper into what we had always taken for granted here at home. Those lawns of carefully kept grass around all Vermont houses, the flower beds of peonies, of roses, of garden pinks, the tall lilac and syringa bushes—so much that costs so little money—are they not a silent declaration of truths we really believe to be self-evident: That there is no reason why people who actually work with their hands should not have their share of the beauty of life as well as anybody—ANYBODY.

How much did Céline take in of what we were trying to tell her? I do not know. I do know that for us our attempted explanation opened new horizons in which the most familiar items of our daily life took on new shape and meaning. Fifty years behind the times, as it may be, we thought, still Vermont is not so bad a place for a European to learn the moving spirit behind the American way of life.

What I present to you here is, it always seems to us, a subject for reflection, one of those illuminating comments on life which, when they come from within life itself, cast a light clearer, more penetrating than the most eloquent expounding of abstract principles.

"Where do the *peasants* live?"

Centuries of European history, three centuries of New England life, two centuries of Vermont life, lying quiet in the past as they do, unfold themselves to our look as we turn our eyes inward on the answer to that question.

Some Things Left Unsaid

All during my childhood I heard from the older people at the breakfast table that they had slept little the night before. I knew beforehand the formulae they would use. So do you, probably. "I didn't close my eyes until two in the morning," was one of them. Or, "From one o'clock on, I heard the clock strike every hour until dawn came." Or, "When I do doze off, it is with one eye open. I can hear a mouse stirring in the wall as if it ran over my pillow." Since I slept from twilight to dawn the swoonlike, unbroken sleep of children, I felt very sorry for them.

Until one summer night when, waking up in my little cot bed in the upper bedroom, I heard a wild screaming from the barn. It sounded so terrible that for a moment I sat up in bed, gooseflesh standing out all over me. When the racing of my heart had slowed down enough for me to listen with my mind as well as with my ears, I realized that the screams came from a mother-hen who was then kept in the barn overnight, because she had a brood of baby chicks who would be safer there than in the hen-house.

As soon as I knew what it was, I raced downstairs in my nightgown and into the south wing where my two aunts slept, the younger, middle-aged one in a small bedroom; the ancient one, the great-aunt, in the main room.

They were both snoring!

I stood on the threshold transfixed. With that hen screaming like a man whose throat was being cut, how was it possible that they could be *sleeping!* Running to my great-aunt's bed, I shook her, shouting, "Oh, Aunt Mary, wake up! wake up! Something terrible is happening to the hen with the chickens." It took some shaking, let me tell you, to wake her.

When she finally sat up, her white nightcap tied tightly under her many chins, her eyes wide-open, we could hear from the bedroom next door a peaceful drone of snores. Aunt Mattie was still asleep! In spite of the hen, in spite of the noise I was making.

Both together, Aunt Mary and I shook and shouted her awake. Then all of us went as fast as we could out to the woodshed. We lighted a lantern. Aunt Mary carried it out to the back yard. The only weapons in sight were the hoe and a rake. Aunt Mattie and I snatched these up. We stepped out into the dew-wet grass, and moved towards the barn.

It was a still, moonlighted summer night, very warm. We had not thought of putting wraps on. Aunt Mary, the lantern held high, went first, immense, rotund in her long, ample nightgown, the peak of her nightcap waggling to and fro as she stepped. Aunt Mattie and I trotted behind her. The hen kept up her appalling screams. Aunt Mary opened the barn door. What we saw there made us start back. The light of the lantern showed us a black and white animal, facing the mother-hen.

A skunk!

That was the only time I ever saw my great-aunt frightened. We were all far more than frightened—we were in a panic! If you have lived in the country you don't need to be told that the only person brave enough not to be afraid of a skunk is somebody who doesn't know about skunks!

We turned tail and ran away. And did we run fast! Aunt Mary was four-square in dimension but she led the retreat, bounding over the grass with the nimbleness of terror.

Her panic was brief. Back at the door to the woodshed she stopped, made an about-face, called a peremptory halt to our rout, and took command. "We can't leave that hen. We've got to help her," she said, getting out the drill-sergeant's rasp in her voice. "We don't need a *lantern!* What possessed us! The moonlight is enough." She set the lantern down. "Now each of us pick up things to throw. We can stand off at a distance, and shout and yell and throw things at the skunk. Maybe we can frighten him off." She leaned forward and took a scrubbing brush from a shelf. Then, seeing the pile of firewood across the woodshed, she dropped the brush. "Oh, Dolly," she said to me, "that firewood will be just the thing. See how many sticks you can carry."

She filled her arms with the sticks of wood, and so did I. Firmly she walked back towards the open barn door. So did I.

I had just dimly perceived that Aunt Mattie was not with us, when her voice came down to us from the open window of my upstairs bedroom. We turned our heads. She had lighted a candle, and holding this over her head was leaning out of the window, calling down to us in an agitated, imploring voice, "Oh Aunt Mary! *Don't* let the skunk get those poor baby chicks! Dolly, quick! Drive him away!"

We were now near the open barn door. The moonlight shone in clear. We could see as if by daylight. And I've never forgotten what we saw. The skunk had fluffed his long-haired coat out threateningly till to me he looked as big as a small bear. To the hen, too, evidently, for her every feather was standing on end, her wings stretched out to the widest. She looked as big as an eagle. And as fierce. Her beady eyes glittered, her sharp, strong, pointed beak was wide-open, and from it came a stream of that astounding screaming which had lifted me out of my bed. She was like a creature gone stark mad, as she stood ragingly against the wild animal threatening her babies. Now I could see that she was slowly, very slowly, advancing. As slowly, the skunk was retreating. Back of him we could see the black hole in the plank wall through which he had entered.

As she thus faced the enemy down, she made sudden venomously-quick jabs at him with her daggerlike beak. Some of her downy yellow chicks were cowering in the straw, feebly cheeping, some were trying to hide under her long, sinewy legs.

"Come on, Dolly!" said my great-aunt. She lifted her arm, threw a stick of firewood at the skunk, at the same time letting out a stream of shrieks and yells that outdid the hen. I threw one, and began to whoop and scream, too. Aunt Mary threw another. So did I. We both screeched like banshees. It was wonderful. Out there in my nightgown at two in the morning, wildly hurling sticks of wood and yelling my head off—did a little girl ever have such an unforgettable adventure.

This flank attack was too much for the skunk, already

daunted. He backed off, swinging his head uncertainly from side to side. Then with the suddenness of a whip cracking, he flashed around and was gone.

"Well—!" said Aunt Mary. She stood an instant to get her breath, then led me in to stop up the hole. Together we pulled some heavy boards across it, piled in front of them some odds and ends of pieces of iron that lay in a corner.

When we turned around we saw that the hen had collected all the frightened chicks and was getting them under her wings. She was talking to them, in a soft crooning, as she lifted and spread her wings to cover them all. Her bristling feathers now lay flat and smooth in their usual decorous Plymouth Rock pattern. Her murmured reassurances had a sleepy lullaby sound, her stupid, low-browed hen-face that had been so like a Medusa's head was calm and maternal. The chicks, worn out by excitement, staggered sleepily on their sticklike legs. As we watched, the last one snuggled his way in under her wings. She drew a long breath and stopped crooning. She, too, was worn out. Her eyes filmed over, shut. She had gone to sleep.

Aunt Mary and I tiptoed out and shut the door as quietly as we could. The old woman said not a word. Neither did I.

Nor did we ever, not once, say anything about how Aunt Mattie got into the house and upstairs. All three of us had been completely panic-struck for an instant. Aunt Mattie's panic had lasted longer than an instant. Panic makes different people act differently. There was no more to say.

As far as not saying anything, I never said anything, either, about the way those "poor sleepers" were hitting the pillow.

Folk-lore

People who live in a big city are constantly rushing to and fro, passing hundreds of people they don't recognize. That is, they see that something is there, on the sidewalk in front of them, but they don't recognize them as fellow-human beings. "They look at you," said a country neighbor of mine, reporting on her first visit to a big city, "the way we look at trees, enough not to run into the trunks."

Of course, in this pouring along of the streams on the streets, every city person, every once in so often, sees a face familiar to him, enough familiar, that is, to call out as they pass, "Hi! *How* are yeh?" And then, like Pilate, stay not for an answer.

It seems to us rustics that, in the course of each day's doings, they come into human contact, really human, with about the same number as we, of men and women and children. But we may be mistaken about this, for they often tell us, commenting on the difference between our lives, that they should think

« 167 »

we'd lose touch with what's going on in the world, isolated from people as we are.

In some respects they are right, of course. We knew vaguely that there is such a thing as the new science (is it a "science" yet?) of carefully observed, professionally analyzed folk-lore. That is, we had seen the name of this new branch of learning in the newspapers. But we hadn't much idea of what it is until a visitor happened into our valley, the friend of a friend, who was a folk-lore specialist. He had dinner with us and stayed through the evening hours and talked a good deal—possibly more than he would in a subway train—about what you find when you really look into folk-lore. We often still think about and talk over what he told us.

To our astonishment, we found what we never dreamed before, that our old stories, just the kind I'm setting down on these pages, are "folk-lore." Like Monsieur Jourdain, astonished to find that he had been speaking prose all his life, we were taken aback to know that we had always been neck-deep in folk-lore without having known it.

One of the things we found out about folk-lore during that long evening of questions and answers was that the erudite in this field hold two bitterly opposed theories about how it gets spread abroad in the world. I find I can't remember the names of the two opposing theories, but I can tell you the two contrasted ideas. We did not even know that the same kind of stories are told by human beings all over the world, not always identical, but very much alike. To think—we often now exclaim over this—that our American Indians often tell their young folks the same kind of tale as can be found, well, in the South Sea Islands or in Scandinavia. One of the theories about this fact is that enormous migrations of people in canoes, or perhaps over land-bridges now submerged, carried the tales from one part of the globe to another. According to this hypothesis, folk-stories were passed around far from their origin by traders, perhaps, or just by people moving.

The other theory is (if I remember accurately and I won't guarantee this) that exactly the same kind of stories springs up from the same kind of circumstances. In other words, many folk-stories are identical in very widely separated geographical places, because all human minds work very much in the same way, and distill from what happens around them, personally, very much the same kind of ideas and legends.

But of course we didn't think at all that this scientific lore concerned us here, in our valley, until—well, I'll tell you about how I chanced to discover to my astonishment that our old stories are folk-lore.

Here is an example of one theory or the other. I've no idea which one it proves or disproves. You choose!

One of the old stories here was of a doctor in the early part of the nineteenth century. We didn't know the doctor for he died some time ago but we know his children and his grandchildren for they are still living in our valley. A very old woman from a back road came in to consult him one evening about a foot which hurt her when she walked on it. She took off her shoe to show him—she had no stocking—and he looked at the foot in horror, for it was as caked with dirt as any barnyard animal. She came from a far back road, you see, and she was very old, and old people find it hard to go through the endlessly detailed procedures of keeping yourself clean. Dismayed and very disapprovingly he said to her, "Heavens, what a dirty foot!" And then, "I'll give you a dollar if you can find another foot as dirty as that in this town."

To which the old woman very cheerfully, and laughing in

his face, snatched the shoe off the other foot and stuck that out, holding out her hand for the dollar.

We know who the old woman was, because the story was reported, from the very evening when it happened in the doctor's office. But when some five or six years ago, I was busy writing about the historical traditions of Vermont, I had occasion to consult a good many records of Vermont outside our valley. And what was my dismay to find that story about the old woman's dirty foot repeated in several towns in Vermont.

Make what you can of that fact. If it hadn't been for our learned folk-lore caller, I really would have been taken aback.

There's another one, too, which I had always heard.

Before I even begin on that one, I'll have to tell you the odd, small item that a rod is sixteen and a half feet long. You probably learned that in your fifth-grade arithmetic book, but it's dollars to doughnuts you don't remember it, for almost certainly you have had no occasion to measure the distance of a line on the ground.

Now you're ready for the story—it concerned an elderly farmer whom my older generation knew very well, and his young, rash son. The young man was out plowing one day, and with the thoughtless imprudence of youth had tied the reins of the horses together and put them around his waist so that he would have both hands free to wrench the plow loose from any root it got into, or pull it around any projecting rock. This isn't considered good practice, and he knew it. But he thought he'd just risk it for once.

Things would have gone very well, if the horses had not stepped into a hornets' nest!

When that story is told here, every detail is recounted, of the wild panic of the horses and their racing madly across the rough field pulling the young plowman off his feet at once but still dragging him along, all mixed up with the plow-share and their hoofs, because the reins were around his waist. You can imagine all that, or rather I suppose none of us can really imagine it. The horses fetched up to a halt finally, with the plow hooked around a tree strong enough to hold them. And the farmer's son in a sorry state of cuts and bruises and broken bones still tangled up with the plow.

His father and the hired man came out running, carried him into the house, rushed off, one of them, on the farm's fastest young horse to get the doctor. The farmer, terrified by his son's condition, sat down sorrowfully by the bed to wait until the doctor came. The boy was unconscious. Presently he opened his eyes a little and saw his father sitting beside him.

The older man said, not unkindly, but just because he couldn't help it, "Son, you oughtn't to have tied them reins around your waist."

To which the son, closing his eyes, said faintly, "Father, I knew I'd made a mistake before I'd been dragged two rods."

This massive understatement has been much used ever since I can remember Arlington stories. When people blunder into some trouble by an error in their own judgment, they often use it as an exclamation. In fact, it is so familiar that it often is not told, the whole of it; the person who has got himself into a mess merely murmurs, "I knew I'd made a mistake—" and lets it go at that.

But in this same research survey of all kinds of Vermont sources, didn't I find *that* story turning up again in several Vermont towns! I can't make it out at all. Can you?

But my astonishment at having lived in the midst of folk-lore all my life without realizing it rose to a peak when I found that an old French story of country life, although not identical in detail, had the same sort of base as one of our own. In each case it concerned the portrayal of the typical muddle-headed yokel in a brief anecdote told by keen-witted neighbors. In France, it is a story told by Normans of a Picard farmer. (Every Norman is supposed to have a lawyer's brains, sharp as a pin.) An old woman of Picardy looking out of her kitchen window saw a neighbor's house in flames. Knowing the owner of the house was plowing in a near-by field, she sent her grandson to tell him of this disaster. The boy raced as fast as he could over the clods of newly plowed earth, stopped the farmer, screaming at him, "Your house is on fire! Your house is on fire!"

The slow-witted Picard stopped his horses, waited a moment till the news had penetrated his mind, look horrified, and then—an idea reaching him dimly—slapped his pocket, felt something in it, and cried out, great relief lighting up his broad, heavy face, " 'T's all right, 't's all right. I've got the key in my pocket."

Well, of course that description of a thick-witted man with slow mental processes could not be told of anybody in Vermont, even a thick-witted person. No Vermont farmer would ever lock his house or know where the key is.

But we have a story of the same color told about the traditional half-witted farm helper, of whom there used to be a few scattered on our farms in the days when half-witted people were not considered so dangerous or such problems as they now are.

On a farm near our house through which the Battenkill River runs, there was great excitement one day. A corpse had been found, a drowned man, washed up in shallow water on a sand-bank there. Any form of violent death is so unheard of a happening in a quiet Vermont neighborhood, that in no time the news had spread around. People had come streaming in from the near-by farms to see who the man could be. But nobody recognized the dead man. The river had evidently been carrying the body for some distance before a shallow place had stopped its floating. The doctor was called who, after an examination, said that the man had been dead for some hours. He superintended the carrying of the body on a farm wagon down to the undertaker.

The excitement had been too great to subside at once. Although the corpse was gone, a knot of men and boys still stood on the river bank discussing this melodramatic happening. A slow-witted helper from a neighborhood farm now came up panting and pushed his way into this group. He looked more than startled and astonished, he looked anxious. And his voice was anxious as he asked tremulously, "Did the man have red hair?"

Astonished at his asking a question, one of the neighbors discussing the matter said, "Yes, he did have."

The moron looked more anxious yet, and asked in a faltering voice, "Did he have on a green shirt?"

Several men speaking at once, and thinking that the newcomer had an explanation, called out, "Yes, he did have."

At this, the other turned very pale and in a panic cried out, "Did he have on buttoned black shoes?"

As it happened, nobody had noticed the shoes especially. Finally one man brought them to mind and after a pause said, "No, they were brown shoes and laced."

At which the slow-witted man struck his two hands together joyfully and cried out, "Oh, then, 'twa'n't me!"

That seems to me some kind of evidence about the way folk-lore stories are spread. But I don't know which side the evidence supports. And I don't know what ever became of that specialist who visited us one evening, so I can't get the news to him.

A Fine Man's
Fine Brains

Textbooks on educational theory have in them many such a phrase as "unrealized psychological and intellectual potentialities." Through their many-syllabled jargon you can get the idea that until people have had a full chance for advanced mental training, you never know—and they never know, either—what kind of brains they have.

Yes, you can get the idea, but clogged with long words on a printed page. Such an idea comes to life only when you—so to speak—*see it happen* in a human life.

James Tynan—his parents were among the first of the wave from Ireland—was one of the finest citizens we ever had in town, and one of the capable and reliable builders. He had learned carpentering by rule of thumb, working with older men who had only rule-of-thumb skill. They all knew how to cut rafters and make stairs, but only because they had learned from their grandfathers, who knew no more than they of abstract theory. Jim Tynan turned out to be the very best practical builder in town. Many of the barns and houses now used in Arlington were built solidly and to last, by Jim Tynan in his young and middle manhood.

He grew up in the nineteenth century, before Arlington had so much as thought of having high-school opportunities for its young people. By the time his oldest daughter finished the eighth grade, the first two years of high-school studies were being provided by the town. The youngsters, in their second year, began geometry for which most of them felt the lack of enthusiasm youngsters generally feel for "math." Early in the school year Mary happened to take her textbook home one day to do her homework. Just before he was ready to go to bed, her father, seeing the book on the corner of the table, picked it up idly and began to turn its pages.

He didn't go to bed. When the rest of them did, he had sat down with the book, calling out to his family, "I'll be up in a minute. I'll just sit up a little while longer and glance through this book."

Next morning, when they all came sleepily downstairs for breakfast, they found their father just turning the last page. He had become so excited by the material in it that he had read steadily all through the night. As he saw his family awake again, he looked up at them, his eyes brilliant. He closed the geometry text, laid it on the table, and said with a long breath, "That's the most interesting book I ever read in my life! It tells me the reasons *why* I do the things in constructing buildings that I've done all my life. Now I understand them."

Then he got up and washed his face and shaved, had his breakfast and went off to work again.

I can just tell you not a person who knew of that night-long rapture of understanding has ever forgotten it.

His son was sent to the Rensselaer Polytechnic Institute, graduated with honors, and has been for many years a very successful civil engineer. Perhaps one may be permitted to exclaim in the naïve phrase of the song often sung by third-graders, "Hurrah for the Red, White and Blue."

In Queen Victoria's
Decorous Days

If you are old enough to have grandchildren, you may have a personal reason for reading the following report on an unimportant incident of everyday long ago. (By that I mean in the nineteenth century.) Or, come to think of it, if you are young enough to have grandparents still alive. For the real theme of the incident is the relationship between young folks and old people at a time when the young were required to show respect to their elders. Note, please, that word "show." Perhaps the title at the top of this page should be, "What do you mean —respect?"

That summer, when the time came for the annual visit paid by their Cousin Mett to the Chipman family, the three Chipman girls were old enough to be young ladies, although only the oldest of the three was over twenty. The Chipman house has always been full of fun, and the three girls contributed their full share to the family enterprise of not taking life too seriously. But they had been brought up to be mannerly, and to show respect to their elders. They made a soberly decorous group when they went to meet Cousin Mett as she came up on the afternoon Flyer (so-called), the once-a-day train which, in those days when Arlington still had a railway, linked Arlington to New York City. Their homemade cotton dresses were fresh and clean and so were their faces.

The train pulled into the station, puffing hard, for the engines on our railway belonged as much to the older generation as did Cousin Mett, and were apt to be out of breath and very glad to stop when they came to a station. Cousin Mett, imposing with age, dignity, and city clothes, appeared at the door of the one passenger coach. The gray-haired conductor came down the steps before her, reached up his hand to steady her descent. But he very carefully kept his eyes on her face, or off to one side looking into the distance, so that any chance disclosure of her feet and ankles which might be made by the wind's blowing of her very wide and very long skirts would not be disquieting to her.

Cousin Mett stepped ponderously down. The three waiting girls welcomed her, using traditional formulae. They kissed her, one of the two younger girls took her satchel, the middle one took her India shawl and carefully folded it over one arm. The third, the one who was past twenty, offered her arm to Cousin Mett. In the course of these maneuvers, they had all said what they were expected to say—that they hoped the trip had not tired her, that they were glad that the day was fair and not rainy, and that they were glad to see her.

This last greeting was more than a formula. The Chipmans had a due family feeling, and would have welcomed Cousin

Mett if she had been shabby. But she was not. The girls were not sorry to have their Arlington neighbors see their fine-looking old city kinswoman.

On her side, Cousin Mett, of course, also had what was called in those days "family feeling." That is, she took for granted that anybody whose kinship to her was even remotely based on biological ties was much closer to her than any human being not in that circle—even when the relationship was, as in this case, only the descendants of one of her mother's second cousins. Also, she was realistic enough to appreciate a welcome in a comfortable home in a cool valley, where, every summer, she could escape from the big house in the hot city in which, since her widowhood, she lived in well-cushioned but rather arid ease. It is quite within the realm of possibilities that, although dignity is always in danger from proximity to youth, she may have felt some warmth from a pleasant reflection of the joy in life of the three Chipman girls.

So, for one and another reason (although by no means the one usually alleged, that "blood is thicker than water") they were glad to be together as the four of them stepped sedately along.

Cousin Mett came from down-country somewhere, I've forgotten just where—New Jersey, Pennsylvania. Her mother had married a "non-Vermonter." Her maiden name was Cope. There aren't any Copes in Vermont. She herself had married a Lippincott. She looked very Cope and Lippincott, too, for she had always had considerably more money than any of her Vermont kin, and ever so much more "presence." Her dresses were, summer and winter, heavy silk, or shining broadcloth, made by a professional dressmaker, her white hair was elaborately waved and puffed, under a skillfully milliner-made hat —none of your countrified amateur improvisations. Mostly she wore black, very dark blue or very dark gray, as became a lady of her age and that period. To cheer up these sober colors, she wore a broad turned-down starched white collar and a spreading silk tie (with white polka dots usually) under her several chins. For Cousin Mett, like other matrons of her time, had never heard of such a thing as dieting.

Her massive bulk was kept in shape, as shape was then thought to be, by iron-clad corsets, laced tightly enough to give her what was then known as "a figure," that is, an approximation to the hour-glass. Without this outline, no woman of good family would be willing to appear on the street.

The little procession started (on foot, of course, no such thing as a cab available) down the hill from the station to our Main Street, where the Chipman house stood.

At this point, I perceive again that the reader being young, at least ever so much younger than I, cannot understand even the tiniest incident from the past without explanations about living conditions of long ago. You won't get the flavor of this whiff from your grandparents' world if I don't tell you about the part played by mud and long skirts in the days when your great-grandparents were old, and living up to their ideal of dignity. Mud was a much more common element in everyday life in those days than in the present. Country roads were practically never paved or hard-surfaced in any way. People walking down from the railway station to our Main Street walked along the side of the road. It was muddy. Not deep mud, you understand, just what is churned up anywhere by passing feet, when Mother Earth is not covered by asphalt or concrete, but is bare to every shower. The two younger Chipman girls walked behind, and the older one with Cousin Mett in front, all of them sincerely glad to be together.

Almost all of every surface in Vermont is tipped, more or

less steeply, up or down. Within ten steps from the railroad station the road began to slope down-hill. Immediately the four ladies, young and old, in a gesture familiar in those days, reached a right hand down and around backward, gathered up some of the folds of their skirts in a firm grip, and lifted the hand just enough (and no more) to raise the hem at the back out of the mud. This gesture was habitual to all femininity, except to very little girl-children whose skirts were short. It was a reflex of which they were not consciously aware. Clutching at their skirts, they continued to walk along, Cousin Mett chatting about the incidents of her long train-trip up from the city. The oldest Chipman daughter beside her listened in respectful silence—and probably, as often happens to those keeping a respectful silence while other people talk, thinking of something else.

The two younger girls, close behind, gazed at the two backs, their sister's slim, flexible, cotton-clad, homemade, the other very much like a broad, firmly overstuffed sofa-back. Their eyes following down the superfluous drapery of the skirt, they noticed that Cousin Mett hadn't gathered quite enough of her full skirt together to be safe. One fold of that costly broadcloth hung so low that with every step, it dipped into the country mud.

I've told you about the omnipresent mud (alternating with dust) of those days. Now I'm sure you will not understand unless I specifically tell you that the combination of long, full skirts and mud had inevitably as result that the hems of those skirts were frequently muddy. Hold it up as they might, ladies could not always achieve two results, both of them of vital importance, self-contradictory by definition—to hold the skirt high enough to keep it all out of the mud, and also to show no inch of their ankles and as little of their feet as possible. For Victorianism, still throwing its shadow from the past into the then present, was convinced that any sight of a woman's nether extremities, feet or ankles (we won't speak of anything else), was far too exciting to men's very excitable senses for a decent woman to risk. (You just should have seen the tremendous columns which upheld Cousin Mett's thickness and breadth, columns enclosed in stout, high, black shoes, buttoned to the top.) It was not only a task to clean the endless length of those hems, but an extremely distasteful one.

Since I seem to have put myself, somehow, in this small tale, into the business of explaining details, now forgotten, of life in the past, I might as well go on and tell you why it was so distasteful. In the days before automobiles, which smell of gasoline, horses were everywhere, and they, too, occasioned a widely distributed smell which, probably, you modern reader, associate with a well-kept stable. For your grandmother (or maybe your great-grandmother), it was all-pervasive. In the mud which clung to those endless yards of hem, there was a good deal of horse-manure as well as disease-laden microbes. The stiff brush dislodging it day after day from the skirt hems filled bedrooms and house with impalpable, almost invisible, filth. Vacuum cleaners had not been invented. The daily process of dusting raised again into the air the dried filth which constantly fell in a fine film upon tables, bric-a-brac, chairs—all of the million surfaces of a well-furnished house in the nineteenth century.

Having been reminded of this one of the good, old ways of the good, old days, you will understand why, when the younger Chipman girls noticed that a part of old Cousin Mett's hem was dipping into the mud as she went down the steep slope of the road leading from the railroad, one of them called out in the Chipman, sunny, good-humored, friendly way, "Cousin Mett, Cousin Mett, your skirt is dragging a little." Her own parents did not exact a cowed and apologetic accent when a younger-generationer made a suggestion to an older person, so she spoke with a natural and casual intonation.

In front of her, the stout monument to the dignity of old age made an instinctive, silent and eloquent reply to the presumptuous claim of a chit to advise an older person how to manage any detail of her life. Cousin Mett opened her hand and let all the yards of that hem drag in the mud behind her, as she swept majestically down the steeply tipped-up road. The Chipman girls had forgotten that Cousin Mett was one of the older generation who was nettled and resentful of any comments from young people.

They took most things mirthfully, and they were not at all cowed by Cousin Mett's wordless rebuke. They looked silently at each other, lifted their shoulders, turned down the corners of their rosy, young lips, spread out their hands and wagged their heads, as if to say, "All right, all right, if that's the way you want it."

This disrespectful pantomime would have been enough of an outlet for their feelings if Cousin Mett had not turned her face, so that it was plainly visible to the girls behind. They were very familiar with Cousin Mett's usual expression of broad, rather complacent dignity. But now it had an added accent of bland self-approval of her skill in successfully putting the innately impertinent younger generation firmly down in its place.

You must remember that those two girls were at the foolish age—oh, the Golden Age!—and that in the teens, there is always, near the surface, that little-girl eruption of deliciously uncontrollable mirth harshly labeled by nettled older people, "the giggles." The combination of Cousin Mett's dignified, self-approving front, and her back, with yards and yards of broadcloth hem sweeping up the mud, was too much for the girls at the foolish age. They burst into giggles.

I hasten to say that of course they did not laugh aloud. They were very nice girls, well brought up to be mannerly and fully understanding that decorum required a surface respect for older people at all moments. They pressed their hands hard over their mouths, their shoulders shaking convulsively, but no sound came from them. Cousin Mett and their older sister walked sedately in front of them, not turning their heads, keeping up the pleasant stream of chat which decorum demanded of members of the same family circle who happened to be together.

The little procession turned into Main Street, where there really were sidewalks, even in those days. Since this was in Vermont, the sidewalks were made of broad slabs of marble (as cheap as any other stone), so that Cousin Mett's well-smeared skirt hem left a light trail of mud behind it. They were soon at the Chipman house. Their mother was watching for them and opened the door to meet Cousin Mett and make her welcome. The two matrons went upstairs together. The girls fled into their own bedroom, flung themselves on the bed, and gave themselves up to an insane and unforgettably enjoyable explosion of the giggles. When their mother came down, they told her the story, and although she made a decent parental show of disapproval, she was swept into the laugh, too.

The Chipman girls adored their mother (occasionally, in those remote, nineteenth-century days, there really was warm affection between members of the family circle) and she not only loved them, but, as they grew up, found them delightful life-companions, improbable as that may sound to modern readers.

But, of course, nobody said anything about it. Not to Cousin Mett, that is. Part of the Victorian conception of human relations was that if you didn't speak about something, it was as good as if it hadn't happened. Well, do you know, now that I have lived on into a period where everybody speaks of anything, there are moments when I feel a little nostalgia for that Victorian pretense?

Two days later was Sunday, and Cousin Mett with all the rest of the family got ready to go to church. She was in her upstairs bedroom dressing carefully before the small mirror which hung between the windows on the front wall. The process of getting into and out of the various complicated garments which are generally worn by what we think of as "civilized people" has been in most periods of history such a complex one, that elderly people usually do most of it by habit, absent-mindedly buttoning, hooking or tying by feel.

Cousin Mett had a certain series of motions, always the same, by means of which she was able to dress almost by reflex. The sequence in which these various steps in the process followed each other was not in the least by chance. It followed the laws of physics precisely. For instance, she always put on her shoes and buttoned them up to their high tops, while her corset still lay on the bed. For if she had put that on, she would not have been able to stoop over to button her shoes. When she had finished buttoning her shoes (she used a button-hook for that process, and as I write the word down, I wonder if any of you younger readers know what a button-hook is), she took up the great Virgin-of-Nuremberg steel armor of her corset. With the skill which came from many years of practice in that art, she got it around herself, hooked all the way up and down her front, till her figure was established. This was not a speedy process, as there was a good deal of flesh and blood to adjust to the fashion.

Now I see I'll have to digress to set down something else intimate about Victorian ladies and their ways. I am recurrently astonished that the most common, everyday elements of life when I was a child are now forgotten. I have told you that Cousin Mett was carefully corseted, to "keep herself in shape" as the phrase went. "The shape" was decreed, not by Mother Nature, but by what was in style, and it was in style to have a distinct inward curve all around the waist. This was hard to manage by very thin women, who used oddly shaped pads to fill out the hollows; but there were not many beanpoles among middle-aged nineteenth-century matrons. Prosperous women, who, like Cousin Mett, seldom made any bodily effort (household help cost so little then that you wouldn't believe it if I told you) and who always had plenty to eat (to put it mildly!), had the wherewithal for any kind of wished-for figure. Whalebone, steel, and stout corset-laces achieved the indentation at the waist by using the corset to push both up and down the flesh which normally belongs around the middle of the human body.

The part which was pushed down made the big hips which were an indispensable element of the then-fashionable "figure." The part which was pushed up became the protruding bosom which, as women grew older and stouter, protruded more and more. In our youth, we took it for granted, but you of the younger generation probably would have stared hard to see such a cylindrical roll sticking out from the upper part of a woman's front. It was carefully compressed so that it should not suggest to the eye any part of a human anatomy—although of course the smallest child knew exactly what was hidden.

A part of the Victorian tradition of decorum was satisfied if a life-element which couldn't be eliminated was made to appear like what everybody knew it was not. This strange protrusion was as skillfully covered, with tightly smooth broadcloth or silk or muslin, as the arm of any sofa.

Now you know, must know from experience and observation, that everybody occasionally lets fall a fragment of food. That's why we have napkins. This minor accident happened to Victorian women with the kind of figure which I have described. But in their case, the crumbs or other tiny particles of food did not fall, as nowadays, upon the plate or napkin-on-the-lap but lodged on the protrusion. Since no decently brought-up man would mention openly, in words, a part of a respectable woman's anatomy, it required some ingenuity for a man to warn a lady of the family circle of the presence of such a crumb. To meet the need, different formulae were invented, by different families. Many's the time I remember hearing one of the serious old relatives of my grandfather's circle, observing that a piece of the breakfast toast had so fallen and lay unnoticed, begin to chant, not looking at the subject of his comment, this jingle:

> "When I was a *boy,*
> I lived by my*self,*
> And all my bread and cheese I *kept*
> Upon the pantry *shelf."*

Nobody laughed, nobody seemed to hear a syllable of this, but the elderly ladies present glanced down and, as if absent-mindedly, one of them daintily brushed off her shelf, while going on imperturbably with their conversation.

Cousin Mett had a bosom so bountiful that, like a great many women of that era, she could not look down over the edge of it. Once she had her corsets on, and the stiffly boned bodice of her dress hooked up, she never could see her front from where what might be called her cornice curled over.

After Cousin Mett's mighty corset was hooked up, she began a series of motions, always the same, performed in a sequence which did not vary because it was adjusted to her bodily capacities. First, she got into the stiffly boned bodice of her dress, and hooked it together in front from under her chin down to what you might call the front edge of her bosom, *not* down to the waist. She couldn't have raised her arms if the bodice had been entirely hooked. Next, she ascertained the exact middle of the necktie as it lay on the dresser, and reached around to pin it with a little safety pin at the back of her bodice. Then she put on her broad starched collar, and fastened that in front, to a button on her bodice which held it down. Her next move was to bring the two ends of the necktie around under the starched collar, and tie it under her chin. But as people get older the sequence of reflex motions is sometimes blurred by momentary forgetfulness.

Cousin Mett, being elderly, was beginning to be a little forgetful. That day she went through the habitual preliminary moves with the necktie, pinned the middle of it in the middle of her bodice in the back, put her collar on and buttoned it up in front. But at that point she noticed in the mirror that a lock of her hair hung loose. Pausing, she pushed it back and pinned it up. This handling of a hairpin shunted her off on a sequence of mechanical gestures beyond the point at which she had arrived. She noticed that her curly false front lay on the dresser, and now undertook, out of its order, the operation of pinning it on. (I don't stop to define what a "false front" is, for if I explained all the details of that period, I'd never get on with what happened.) It was essential to have one's false front pinned squarely in the middle of the forehead, for the least tip to one side or the other had a comic effect, very damaging to dignity. She looked carefully in the small mirror while she pinned it in place, shifted it several times, and finally got it, she thought, settled. This had taken her a little longer than usual. At this point she heard the church bell clanging out its last call to morning service. So she knew it was almost time to leave the house.

Forgetting that she had one necktie pinned already at the back of her bodice and hanging down there, she hastily took another one out of the drawer, pinned the middle of that at the back and brought it around to the front, tying it in one of her flowing bow-knots. She did this in a hurry, and being in a hurry is fatal to exactitude of movements on the part of old people. Having passed, in the mechanical sequence of operations, the time when she should have hooked together her bodice from the edge of her shelf down to her waist, she forgot that she had not done it.

So that when the Chipman girls, standing at the foot of the stairs, all ready to go to church and waiting for Cousin Mett, looked up, they saw her, majestic in her expensively fine dark brown broadcloth dress, coming down the stairs with her usual slow dignified step, her bodice unfastened below the jutting curve of her bosom, not hooked from there down to the waist at all and hence exposing to view her clean, starched and well-ironed corset cover. I know you never saw one of these garments, but I am not going to describe it to you. You can guess what it was from its name. As the three Chipman girls gazed spell-bound at Cousin Mett, holding firmly to the railing of the stairs, and coming slowly down towards them like a ship under full sail, they observed furthermore that she had on two neckties—one, a pink one, flowing broadly down the middle of her back, and another, dark blue with white stripes, tied in a bow under her collar in front.

What do you suppose those naughty girls did? They never opened their mouths. Remembering how they had been snubbed and put in their places two days before, coming down the hill from the railway station, they kept a wicked, demure, wide-eyed silence.

To tell the truth, they were literally overcome by the epic dimensions of what was happening. Cousin Mett, very erect (those corsets always made women erect), composed, sure of herself as only the older generation of those days (when prosperous) could be sure of themselves, nodded an indulgent greeting to her little country relatives, and swept on past them out of the Chipman front door and along the marble sidewalk towards the church.

Beside her, looking as though butter wouldn't melt in their mouths, walked her little country relatives in such an inner turmoil as they scarcely ever again felt. Cousin Mett's broad elderly face was set in its usual expression of composed certainty that her family was as good as the best and she a wholly worthy member of it.

The girls were not giggling. They were scared. Their prank, if it could be called that, was far too serious. They had not at first taken in how serious! Suppose they met someone on the sidewalk who—what ever in the world would people in church *do,* when they—

But they met nobody at all in the short walk over the sidewalk. Nor was anybody in the vestibule of the church when they stepped in. Everybody was already inside, in his pew.

As they came in, they could hear—if you could call it hearing—the before-service hush inside the church. Then through the swinging doors came the rector's voice, slow and sonorous, *"I was glad when they said unto me—."* In the silence around the familiar words, they could hear the rustle of the congregation, as they began the well-known sequence of the morning service—everybody standing up and opening his prayer book at the right place.

"Let the words of my mouth—" the rector's voice went on. In the echoingly empty vestibule the Chipman girls literally quaked.

Cousin Mett let go the clutch of her right hand on her skirt behind, let it fall, and shook out its expanse till its folds hung in their usual stately lines clear down to the floor.

"Let all the earth keep silence," the rector's voice boomed out through the crack between the swinging doors.

It was not the Chipman girls who were breaking any silence. Like panic-struck mice, they scarcely breathed. If they could have had their way, the floor of the vestibule would have opened and let them down into the basement of the church. But it did not—when does it ever?

They were now flustered out of their senses. This could not be happening, not really!

Cousin Mett, imposing (in spots), held her head up and with the certainty of her generation that youth would follow wherever age led, she pushed open the swinging doors and stepped into—

But a sudden chill comes over me. This story is not for modern readers.

I'm wasting my time in trying to tell it to you. Since you can't have the slightest idea of what decorum was and what it meant, how could you possibly feel how horrifyingly comic was a break in it? You couldn't.

Let the Bridges
Fall Down

Town Meetings are important events in any Vermont town. Once in a while, there is one which the community never forgets, because in it a crisis was reached and passed. One such came in Arlington as the ending of years of effort to build a graded school.

Till then, we had had district schools scattered all around the township, as was the old way of providing educational opportunities. Children lived then in homes very much more widely separated than now. For instance, up on what is called Southeast Corners, where there isn't now a single house or even a cellar hole left, there was quite a sizable settlement in the early days. More than thirty children learned to read and write and do their sums in the schoolhouse, and a lively community of active young people lived all around them. But little by little, after the building of the railroad, homes became more and more concentrated down in the valley near the three established settlements of Arlington, East Arlington and West Arlington. The schools in the settlements never had been more than big district schools, poorly equipped, nearly always very much overcrowded. The only education they could offer was a primitive and scanty preparation for American life, which grew constantly more complex. The educational requirements for success in the modern world were ever so much higher than in the old days.

It took a long time for Arlington to recognize the need for a new, well-equipped school if its children were to have a fair chance. Everybody was startled by the high cost of such education. Year after year, the proposition was voted down by one of the two kinds of opinion which always exist in every human group. On one side was the feeling that the status quo—the old, venerated, community-life pattern—must not be touched. "What was good enough for my grandfather is all right for anybody. *He* got along all right." These citizens represented the natural human love for the past. Also the natural human dislike for taxes. Against them were the citizens who hoped that the future would be better than the past. Such voters always struggle to help bring the future to birth, rather than to coast along protecting the way of life of years gone by. Year after year, spirited discussions were held, as these two elements in our community fought—with ballots, the American way—for their idea of what was the best thing to do for our town.

The proposition was to erect a graded school where the primary education would be improved, and which would also provide high-school education. Till then, the nearest high school had been in North Bennington. There were few automobiles, the roads were not left open in winter, North Bennington was too far for horse-transportation. The only way to reach that nearest high school was by very slow, very inconvenient train service. This meant that of our Arlington children none except those of the relatively well-to-do could get a high-school training. Would it be possible to give them, here in Arlington, the chance for a preparation for life which other American children had? One group of our voters believed that the town could never raise the money for the building and upkeep of the school. They admitted that, from the long-range point of view, better education was needed; but against that need were listed Arlington's immediate wants. The hill roads should be resurfaced. Care for the sick poor was more costly every year. But above all the bridges.

Our bridges needed reinforcement not only from recurring flash floods and high water but against the increasing tonnage of modern traffic. It would take all the tax money we could raise to keep the bridges in repair; and there were many other absolutely necessary material needs. It would be simply crazy to add to our spending the enormous (so it seemed to us) cost of a new school.

The discussion was hot. The material needs of the body, and the immaterial needs of the mind and spirit, stood up to see which was the stronger. As often happens, the material needs outshouted the need for human development and growth. They sounded much more actual and real.

The little flickering flame of responsibility to protect the future of the town's children grew dimmer. Those who had, year after year, worked for a good school sat silent. The predicted crashing of the bridges sounded loud in their ears. What could be said against *that?*

Then up sprang Patrick Thompson. What education he

had—such as it was, was sound—he had received in our meager district school. And he knew that it was not enough for his children.

We usually saw him in a white apron standing behind the counter in his grocery store selling sugar and tea. We have never forgotten how he looked that day at Town Meeting, his powerful shoulders squared, his hands clenched. I still remember his exact words, intense as the flame of a blowtorch. "We are being told," he said, "that our town cannot afford to keep its bridges safe and also make a decent provision for its children's education. That's what we are being *told*. Not one of us here really believes it. We just can't think of anything to say back. But suppose it were true—then I say, '*If we have to choose,* let the bridges fall down!' What kind of a town would we rather have, fifty years from now—a place where nit-wit folks go back and forth over good bridges? Or a town which has always given its children a fair chance, and prepares them to hold their own in modern life? If they've had a fair chance, they can build their own bridges. You know which of these two is really wanted by every one of us here. I say, 'If we have to choose, *let the bridges fall down!*'"

He took his seat in silence.

It was the turning point in the life of our town. We knew it was. So we spoke not a word but sat thinking. When the vote was taken, a big majority voted "yes" for the school. Some years later, that school—not very well built—burned and was replaced, almost without an opposing vote, by a better one. The whole town had moved forward by a long step.

Patrick Thompson has been long in his grave. But he walks at the head of every graduating class in our high school.

This story was written just as it happened, and put into *Vermont Tradition*. From that book it has been taken out to be reprinted in ever so many newspapers and magazines and books all across the United States. And it has been translated and published in magazines in France, in Portugal, in Spain, and in Japan.

Think of our Arlington citizen shouting out his cry for better education—in Japanese!

Henry LaBatt's Stroke

Arlington of the twentieth century has not at all lost its habit of turning small everyday chance happenings into a good-humored laugh, which passes around and around the community and ends by leaving in our minds—well, what? Perhaps each one ends by giving us a little more accurate idea of how life affects human beings.

Only last summer Henry LaBatt (he and his wife, both now elderly members of my own age group, live in what was the old Lawyer Harmon Canfield house) walked up to the barber shop between the two villages to get his hair cut. He's not very well, and it seemed like quite a distance; but it was a pleasant summer day and the errand not a disagreeable one. Having your hair cut by the barber is apt to be a social event with a chance to talk over neighborhood news with other men waiting for their turn in the barber's chair. Laying down his hat and cane and taking off his glasses, Henry sat down for a pleasant chat with some neighbors. Before his turn for a haircut came, he had had time to hear the latest news and to talk some politics. After his hair was cut, he started home, in very good spirits.

But when he reached the house after this he was in a dreadful state. Wavering on unsteady feet, stepping high, leaning hard on his cane, he barely managed to get up on the porch, staggered into the living room, took off his hat and glasses, let his cane drop and sank down on the couch, white-faced and dizzy. "Something awful's happened to me," he said solemnly to his wife. "I don't know what! But something terrible. My *mind's* not right. The ground has been coming right up to me all the way home. And now I feel *sick*—seasick, you know. Do you suppose I've had a stroke!"

His wife was alarmed. She hovered over him anxiously, took his pulse which was normal, took his temperature which was normal. She sat down perplexed, beside the couch. "Perhaps you got too tired," she said. "It's quite a walk from here up the hill to the barber's. Do you feel anything *queer* anywhere?"

"No," Henry said. Now that he was lying down, the unearthly feelings of total uncertainty of everything—the strange symptoms—dizziness, seasickness—they all seemed to be fading away.

Much cheered, his wife said, "Maybe you'll be all right after you've had a rest."

So he lay there quietly. He really felt much better. They were both relieved, thinking that the attack, whatever it had been, might have passed away. He reached again for his cane and glasses and stood up on his feet, but cried out at once that it was worse than ever. He staggered wildly, almost lost his balance. Now the floor rose up in waves, and the walls of the room spun around. He reeled so that his wife caught at him and steadied him, as he fell, so that it was on the sofa that he once more collapsed. She was really alarmed now and said anxiously, "Look, Henry, this is something *very* serious. Take my arm. We'll go right across the street and ask Dr. Russell."

But as, arm in arm, they started towards the door, they saw that a little boy was standing there. He had been knocking, but in their agitation they hadn't heard him. He held up his hand with something in it. "Here are your glasses, Mr. LaBatt," he said. "The barber said you took somebody else's by mistake when you left the shop."

Not a year has gone by since that absurd little episode, but already it has shown itself no mere dry pebble, no mere comic anecdote. Like others which we repeat laughingly, it has turned out something living, a root which has begun to sprout meanings beyond the incident itself. It is one of our footnotes on life. Just the other day I heard somebody say impatiently, "Seems to me that the children nowadays aren't anything like as bright as they used to be when I was young. Nor as reliable! Makes me sick to see how foolishly they carry on."

A man who was with him said neutrally, "Maybe you've got on those glasses Henry LaBatt wore away from the barber shop."

A Stranger, an Outsider

Before Ernest Kent retired from his profession and came with his family to live in Arlington, they had almost certainly heard (everybody does hear this) that Vermonters are provincial-minded rustics, absolutely closed to those from other states. We note that such newcomers often say, with the assured accent used for an accepted axiom, "In this kind of town, the natives always hold you off at arm's length. To them, no matter how long you live here, you can never be anything but an outsider, a stranger."

When Ernest Kent (Dr. Kent was what we usually called him, respectfully) came with his family to live in Arlington, he was, for sure, an outsider to us. And you might have thought he'd be a formidable outsider, for he had a distinguished air about him, had been very successful in his profession, had a Ph.D. in education, was retiring from a lifetime of active, successful service as a high executive in the

Department of Education in a large, modern city. Nothing more different from our small Vermont community could be imagined.

And he certainly was a stranger to us all.

Well, in no time, Ernest Kent was one of the most highly prized citizens of Arlington, known to everybody, young and old. We would have been amazed if he had ever been called "an outsider." It was not that we thought of him as a "native." We just thought of him as "Dr. Kent." And that was enough!

We were far too unskilled in professional "social techniques" to perceive the deftness with which he set up his lines of communication with our community life. To us he seemed just to step up on Arlington's front porch and sit down with the family. But, now that he is gone, and we think back over his all too brief years with us, we can see that, from the very first, his "technique" of folk-sharing is open to anybody.

To begin with, he attended meetings!

You know, every American knows, how many "meetings" it takes to keep the wheels moving of our complicated mechanism of voluntary associations for the public welfare. He began where anybody could begin, with P.T.A. meetings. They are open to all, and alas! avoided by almost as many as they are open to. Dr. Kent, from the first, attended every one, listened attentively to discussions, occasionally took a hand in them, drawing on his long experience with schools. And there he began another practice which carried him rocketlike to the center of Arlington activities:

He served on committees!

You know the usual formula when a committee is to be appointed by the chairman: a veil of uneasy gloom settles on the room as the chairman looks around at the gathering and says hesitantly, pausing before the least reluctant-looking face,

"Perhaps Mrs. Hancock would serve?" Mrs. Hancock usually produces one of several well-worn formulae, "Oh, I don't believe I *could*. The children have been exposed to measles and I couldn't be sure I could leave them." Or, "I'm very sorry but I'm not a bit well this winter and the doctor doesn't want me to...." Or, in the case of a man, "My work at the office takes just all I've got."

Dr. Kent always answered with alacrity, "I'll be glad to serve. First time in my life I have no long regular working hours. Count on me." Can you imagine the electrifying effect of such an announcement? I'll warrant you haven't heard it very often in your lifetime.

If you know anything about the grapevine-communication service of a small rural group, you don't need me to tell you that by breakfast time the next morning everybody had heard about Dr. Kent. And you can imagine that when the old gentleman (he once happened to mention to me that he and I had been doing graduate work at Columbia the same year, so I know he must have been my age—which is venerable) next appeared at the door of a meeting, perhaps at the Community House, or where the Public Health Service was meeting, somebody sprang up to get him a chair and everybody made him feel welcome.

He not only served on committees, he always accepted assignments for carrying out community activities. Was there need for transportation to get Arlington school children to dental chairs in our shire-town some fifteen miles away, or in summer to a big pond in the other direction for swimming lessons, or was a car needed to take delegates from one of our churches up to a gathering at Montpelier? Dr. Kent was always available. Children and adults loved to go with Dr. Kent because he was so genial, so cheerful, "such *fun*," the children said. We had not noticed till then that in our modern world-on-wheels a long drive in the same car with somebody gives the same opportunity to get acquainted with him as, in old times, a quiet talk before the home hearth fire. More opportunity indeed, because everybody in those crowded automobile rides with Dr. Kent had something in common to begin with, which flowered into friendly intimacy as the long miles flowed under his wheels.

It was but a step for Dr. Kent to advance from these friendly relations with hard-working adult citizens to a unique helpfulness for children of the younger teen-age group. You'll hardly believe it, but what this elderly and not very robust man did for them was to teach them sports. In the course of his service to young people in the big city he had acquired a professional skill in coaching athletics. Now of course he was much too old for the conventional kind of coaching. Yet within a few years from his arrival in our town he had large classes of children learning how to play tennis. Most coaches are not at all gifted in orderly analysis and explanation, and hence they are obliged to show, muscularly, in action, the right way to handle a tennis racquet or to stand on skis. But Dr. Kent had a highly trained mind, skilled precisely in analysis and explanation. This is the way he managed coaching: he stood or sat in a chair at the side of the court in tennis, and with the most ingenious teaching he succeeded in starting the young people off in the right style. Hour after hour he watched these beginners, told them just how to hold the racquet, and called out such admonitions as, "Don't face the net! Always keep sideways to it." "Don't run up on the bounce." "Reach up!" "Always keep the ball ahead of you." "Loosen up!" "Swing freely, don't try to push the ball, *hit it!*" "Do your hurrying with your mind, not with your legs." The best teaching he did was the unexpressed (in words) but plainly understood and grasped axiom that games are played not only to beat the other fellow but to acquire skill—to beat yourself.

He taught skiing to our younger generation in very much the same way, first taking the infinite pains, necessary in a plain rural community, to see that the children and young people he was instructing had the necessary equipment of passable skis, passably waxed, of bindings that would hold, and poles of the right length. Well muffled up from the cold, he stood halfway down the practice slope, watching keenly the wavering young skiers as they passed, shouting out axioms like those of any professional ski teacher—being mostly comprised of variations on the basic themes of "Bend your knees!" "Keep your weight *forward!*" "Bend your knees but don't squat." "Stand up but lean forward."

He let himself be elected as Town Tree Warden—a very minor official post sedulously avoided by most citizens. And what a Tree Warden he was! We had not dreamed that this position could be so useful. He acted as informal, unpaid— but invaluable—"vocational advisor" to any high-school senior who needed steering. Like any other time-seasoned, expert educator he knew more than any of us about when to give advice, and when to tell a funny story, and when to open the door to the inner room where real life goes on. It was astonishing how much more smoothly our local affairs ran with Dr. Kent at hand, using his superiority, as he did, to help us, not to overawe us. How we missed him when he and his wife went off for a winter vacation.

On one of these vacations he died. He was an old man. The news did not surprise us, but it shocked us. When the telegram came back to Arlington, the sorrowful phrase which ran from houses in the village and along the wires of the party-line telephones in the farming districts was, "How will we ever manage without Dr. Kent!" The date for the annual Town Meeting fell soon after his death. Before the assembled citizens there, the Moderator read a detailed statement of appreciation of the services to our town of this "outsider," this "stranger." By unanimous vote, it was decided to have this placed permanently on record by having it printed in our Town Report —something not often done. In the center of our village an evergreen tree was planted to honor his memory.

Ever so many things in the seasonal round of our communal life remind us of Dr. Kent. But he is so vividly present in our hearts at one special event that we can almost see him there with us, grizzled, a little bent, with his friendly smile. This is on the late afternoon every December, just before Christmas, when Arlington children and their parents gather around Dr. Kent's tree, as we always call it, for the annual singing of Christmas carols. The early winter twilight falls as we sing. Lights come on in the windows of the near-by houses, shining out golden over the snow. We look up at Dr. Kent's tree and think that it is as green as his memory.

The Soldier's Return

Sandy Welsh was hired man on my great-uncle's farm, just below our house—the Brick Farm House farm. But to put it this way will give you quite the wrong idea of what he was to Uncle Niram and Uncle Niram to him. For "hired man" in Vermont, particularly in the middle of the nineteenth century, does not mean at all what it means in some places and in some times. Sandy was an Irish boy, lovable, steady, hard-working, competent, and my Uncle Niram was a childless farmer, with a very warm heart. To him, Sandy brought to the farm a breath of youth and warm vitality, which was very comforting to an old farmer who had no children of his own. And Sandy felt for "Mr. Niram" the love a nephew might feel for his uncle. Here in the country, you see, an affection can exist like that felt in a family even when there is no blood kinship. We think it's rather nice to have older and younger people feel that way about each other. And when I say "rather nice," I am using Vermont understatement.

Uncle Niram's farm is a big one, and in his day he had, as part of the farm's working equipment, a saw-mill run by the lively brook. Here logs were sawed into boards and a plain kind of woodwork was manufactured for the inside of houses. So of course one helper could not begin to do the work needed, in the mill and on the farm. Although Uncle Niram had no children, and was a widower, his working family, if you can put it that way, had six or seven people in it more or less, off and on. Sandy was at that time much the youngest one, and a favorite with all of them.

You can see that when he decided to enlist as a soldier in the Union Army, very young indeed, it was a blow to everybody. Nobody expected to see the lad come back again alive. Indeed, he was wounded twice, but not severely. And he did come back.

He was mustered out at the end of the war. Somehow he did not have to wait as long as many of the soldiers did to get through the red tape which ties up a discharge from any army. Soon after the end of the shooting, at the ending of the Civil War, his papers came through unexpectedly, in time for him to leap aboard a north-bound train. But not so unexpectedly that some conscientious bureaucrat in an office didn't know about his discharge and sent a telegram up to Uncle Niram that Alexander Welsh was coming home on such and such a day.

Hence it happened that Sandy had no idea that people on the farm knew that he was returning, or which day he was coming. As the train left New York and came north along the Hudson, he thought he was going to surprise them all. At that time, naturally, everything was mixed up in railroad schedules, and he missed connections at Albany so that it was not the afternoon express but the slow evening train which brought him up into our valley.

I've heard the rest of the story from Sandy, whom I knew when I was a little girl. He was then a strongly built, vigorous, elderly man. It was also a favorite story of Uncle Niram's. So I know that as the hour drew near for the arrival of the evening train at Sunderland (the little way-station north of Arlington, and nearest to the farm), Uncle Niram had the whole farm family ready in decent clothes to make a sort of celebration of meeting their returned soldier boy. They climbed into the big farm wagon and started on the two-mile slow drive over the narrow dirt road to the Sunderland station.

In the meantime, Sandy was leaning from the platform of the north-bound train, watching his own valley come into view. You'd better believe there were no vestibule connections between cars in those days, and to stand on the platform meant that you were out-of-doors, in the home wind. The train did not rush north—trains were slower in those days, many of the locomotives in Vermont still burning wood. The dusk gathered as Sandy gazed with all his eyes. He used to say, "It didn't seem possible—it didn't seem *possible!*—that there I was, alive, all in one piece, coming up our own valley."

Of course, he knew, as we all know, every line and dip of the mountains' silhouette against the sky, every slightest bend of the railway line which brought a new field into view, he knew every house, every turn in the dirt road which runs beside the railroad for much of the way.

He continued to stand out on the platform because he couldn't bear to sit indoors where he saw less. At the Arlington station, where the train halted briefly, he saw some people he knew and eagerly waved his hand to them. They had no idea who he was—the soldier in the worn blue uniform. He had grown taller during his absence, and was very thin. As the train moved on from Arlington, every tree and bush and rock was like an old friend to him.

The train inched its way north until it approached the turn, well known to us who go back and forth over the road. We call it "the crossing." Here a side road crosses, and runs side by side with the track for a short distance. Here the engine always gives two loud whistles. Sandy was nineteen years old, reckless with much experience of danger, his heart beating fast to see Red Mountain looming up there just where it always had been. When the whistle gave its two familiar shrieks at the crossing, a crazy notion took the boy that he would just drop off the train and walk the short distance to the farmhouse.

So he did, swinging off with the resilience and exact timing of powerful, hardened, nineteen-year-old muscles. He stumbled a little as he struck the earth, but caught himself before he fell.

There he was, standing on the sound, hard Vermont gravel, instead of the Southern mud where, it seemed to him, he had been slogging ever since he had left home. The train rumbled on. The twilight was deepening. Through it he caught, for the first time, the home smells, the resinous fragrance from the Wyman pines across the tracks, the hemlock odors from the lot to his left as he walked forward, carrying his little bag. On his right was the swamp. Springtime had wakened the frogs—the peepers were out, shrilling in their high, sweet treble as he went by.

When speaking of this, he never told me that he shed some tears there, but I always did at that point when I heard the story.

Just beyond the swamp, the Brick Farm House comes into

view. To his surprise, it was all dark. Not a candle lighted in it. Wondering a little, but thinking that perhaps they were at the back of the house, he stepped forward faster and faster. On the old bridge over the Battenkill, he stopped a moment and leaned on the railing to look down at the black water below, and to listen to the faint stealthy rustle the river makes where the water is deep. This had been one of his favorite swimming holes. He lifted his head and looked around him, divining the darkness of the mountains against the darkening sky. He used to say, "Not a light was to be seen. Not a sound. How black, and grand and lonely it looked."

The little girl listening saw and heard more vividly than ever in her life the raucous, loud, never-silenced swearing and shouting of men's voices, and the incessant rumbling of artillery caisson-wheels and army wagons—saw the smoky flames from bivouac fires which had always glared around the Vermont farm boy in his war years.

He turned into the path that led up to the farmhouse. A dog lay on the porch—yes, just like Ulysses' dog, only Sandy didn't think of that, I suppose. And like Ulysses' dog when he heard the familiar step and the familiar voice, he raised himself up on his fore-paws and thumped his tail on the porch floor. At this point, a knot in the throat of the listening little girl.

But when Sandy opened the door, for of course that Vermont door was not locked, not a soul there. He was in the kitchen, the heart of the home life. It smelled of burning birch bark, of soap, of creosote in the chimney, of geraniums on the window sill, of cookies in the pantry.

"No, it is not possible," he said to himself. "This must be a dream." He would wake in a moment, he thought, and smell burnt gunpowder and men sweating in heavy wool uniforms. These were dream smells.

Sandy couldn't imagine where everybody had gone. This was a very different homecoming from what he had imagined. He walked around, calling. No one answered. Then he thought he would go on up the road to the barn. After all, the barn was his particular workshop, for he took care of the cows.

He left his flat little bag in the living room of the farm-house, and walked up the road. The barn was black, of course. Feeling more than ever that he was sleep-walking, he lifted the heavy wooden latch and let himself in to the warm black-ness, filled with barn odors. The fragrance of hay, the pungent, living odor of well-kept cows. But without as much smell of manure as he remembered. He could hear the cows munching in the darkness, and moving around a little, so he knew that the barn was still full of life. He wondered if the lantern hung on its usual peg. He felt his way along the barn wall until he came to the peg. Yes, there the lantern was. Of course. Why should it be changed? Nothing was ever changed. He lighted the candle which stood inside it, hung it back on the peg and looked around him.

How clean the barn was! He did not know that the entire farm family had turned out to clean it and to brush the cows down, as part of his welcome home. But, as he looked, he thought, I haven't seen a hospital all during the war as clean as this barn. The cows, munching away on their hay, turning their eyes shining in the light of the candle, looked at him without surprise.

He took off his soldier's cap with its hard visor, loosened his military tunic, and drew a long, deep breath. He *must* be dreaming.

The cows stood still in their places but on the other side of the barn a shadow moved. A gray cat came boldly across the floor. A young cat. But Sandy thought, Must be one of Old Fighter's kittens. Those black markings are the same. The cat came up to him, rubbing against his leg and waving his tail. To Sandy he spoke familiar language. He's asking for some milk, he thought, the dreamlike feeling deepening.

"I'm probably sound asleep back in camp," he thought.

But he stooped down and stroked the furry back which arched itself under his hand. "All right, kitty," he said aloud. "We'll get some milk." The three-legged stool stood where it always had, a milking pail near it. He drew the stool up to the nearest cow and began to milk.

He dug his head into the cow's warm, hairy flank, his fingers closed around the yielding, soft, firm tissue of the teats. The streams of milk began to thrum down into the pail. His hands, his big, strong soldier's hands, hardened by carrying arms, seemed scarcely under his control, seemed to act of themselves as they began masterfully to press the teats with the familiar gesture he was proud of doing well. Now it seemed to him he had not been away at all. It was everything that had passed that was the dream—the nightmare.

During this time, the farm family had arrived at the unlighted Sunderland way-station, and sat in the wagon waiting for the train to stop. But it did not stop. It rattled its noisy way past without even slowing down.

Well, the people in the farm wagon thought, Sandy must somehow have missed the train. Or perhaps a mistake had been made by the person who had telegraphed them. Disappointed, and a little anxious for fear something had happened to the boy, they turned the horses' heads, and plodded back to the farm. As they came down the road near the farmhouse, to their surprise, they saw a light in the cow barn. Who in the world could that be? It did not occur to them that it might be Sandy. He could not possibly have come in from the other direction. Uncle Niram said they'd better drive on down to the farm, change from their best clothes to their everyday ones, while he would walk back up to the barn to see who was there.

As he approached, the natural idea came to his mind that a neighbor had been going by, had heard, perhaps, a cow in distress and had gone in to help her. Then, in his turn, he lifted the big, wooden latch, opened the door and stepped in.

There sat a man in a blue uniform, on the milk stool, leaning his head against the cow's flank while the streams of milk drummed into the pail, watched by a waiting cat. As Uncle Niram's old eyes grew used to the dim light of the candle in the lantern, he could see who the man was. It was Sandy. His boy, come back alive from the furnace.

Sandy had heard the door open and felt the breath of fresh air on his cheek. Just as the old dog on the porch had recognized him in the dark, he knew who it was who had come in. But he did not turn his head. Uncle Niram could see, in the dim light, that the tears started from under his downcast lids, and ran down his thin, young cheeks in a glistening stream. Uncle Niram's knees bent a little under him and he leaned back against the barn wall. There was a silence.

It was no dream. The war was over.
"What did you do, Uncle Niram?" asked the little girl.
"Oh, I just cried, too," said Uncle Niram.

172/7